"The four writers, Kierkegaard, Dostoevsky, Nietzsche, and Kafka, occupy, each in his own peculiar
way the position of outsiders in the society that had
produced them. They lived the insecure existence of
spiritual frontiersmen who no longer fit into the accepted categories of theology, philosophy or *belles-
lettres,* and can see during their lifetime no immediate
chance for getting the hearing they deserve. They
realized that they were both the end products of a
dying civilization and the clairvoyant prophets of
coming chaos. Kierkegaard's judgment of himself as
an 'enigma' and Kafka's self-characterization as 'an
end or a beginning' pertain to all four.

"Their contemporaries dismissed their dark premonitions as exaggerated, unbelievable, or outright
fantastic. . . . Kafka was resigned to the coming
triumph of evil, which the other three had also considered a powerful threat or the alarm-signal for
rallying counter-energies. But Kierkegaard, Dostoevsky, and Nietzsche expected a new phase in mankind's history to rise that would fulfill their spiritual
visions, a kingdom to follow disasters of apocalyptic
dimensions. Their emphasis on evil marks them as
eschatological writers."

—from the chapter entitled

"The Four Apocalyptic Horsemen"

Dostoevsky, Kierkegaard, Nietzsche, and Kafka

FOUR PROPHETS OF OUR DESTINY

WILLIAM HUBBEN

COLLIER BOOKS

Macmillan Publishing Company

NEW YORK

COLLIER MACMILLAN PUBLISHERS

LONDON

Preface

THIS STUDY ATTEMPTS to introduce the reader to four of Europe's most mysterious writers—Kierkegaard, Dostoevsky, Nietzsche and Kafka. All four have contributed to shaping the modern mind and have exerted an influence upon Western thinking that is only now beginning to be recognized in its full dimensions. The spiritual crisis which they foresaw with an uncanny sense of clairvoyance and which their own work has greatly intensified, is the root cause of the social and political anxieties of our present time. Their individual profiles are markedly different, yet the continuity of their thinking and the frequently surprising identity of their diagnoses are disturbing our generation as much as their specific prophecies, prophecies which have in large measure come true.

Each of them transcends the boundaries of theology, philosophy, poetry, and psychology to challenge with his appalling message the whole realm of human existence. It is, of course, more than tempting to devote a considerably larger space to any one of these four writers, but the purpose of this essay is to view them as spiritual relatives against the background of a formerly self-assured society which is now in the agonies of a new orientation.

The appended suggestions for further reading are not meant to represent an exhaustive bibliography. The reader will have to make his own discoveries in this vast field of literature. I have refrained from documenting quotations because they have been almost entirely taken from literature in foreign languages. But most of the works of Kierkegaard, Dostoevsky, Nietzsche, and Kafka are now available in English translations.

I am greatly indebted to Mildred A. Purnell, Associate Editor of the "Friends Intelligencer," and Edwin E. Aubrey, Professor of Religious Thought, University of

Pennsylvania, for the care and interest with which they read the finished manuscript and for their critical suggestions.

Philadelphia,
Pennsylvania

W. H.

Contents

Sören Kierkegaard

Truth is a power. But one can see that only in rare instances, because it is suffering and must be defeated as long as it is truth. When it has become victorious others will join it. Why? Because it is truth? No, if it had been for that reason they would have joined it also when it was suffering. Therefore they do not join it because it has power. They join it after it has become a power because others had joined it.

Chapter 1

THE COPENHAGEN STREET urchins used to shout after Sören Kierkegaard "Either—Or," the title of his two-volume work. Copenhagen's satirical paper *The Corsair* printed not only the most merciless articles against him but also published a series of cartoons depicting him successively as a magisterial hunchback; a thin-legged star gazer; a clumsy horseman riding Pegasus; a shadow in the center of a chaotic universe; a rooster with a top hat, surrounded by cackling chickens also wearing top hats; and each time vitriolic satire accompanied these cartoons. Copenhagen, the little Paris of the North, relished both the stories and the pictures. Kierkegaard's thin legs and crumpled pants had become proverbial, and there was nobody who opposed this cruel, "negative conspiracy," as Kierkegaard called the campaign against himself. Goldschmidt, the clever editor of *The Corsair*, had refused any apologies or retractions. Yet only six days after Kierkegaard's death in 1855, when Goldschmidt was no longer connected with *The Corsair*, he wrote that Kierkegaard was one of "the greatest minds Denmark has ever produced."

These attacks were in part the reaction of a self-satisfied and uninformed middle class to the presence of a genius of Kierkegaard's proportions. The citizens of Copenhagen were incapable of imagining that such an extraordinary man could ever rise from the quiet and perfectly proper atmosphere of their town. They saw in Kierkegaard a threat to the order which they loved as final; Hans Christian Andersen described this way of life very characteristically in one of his stories when he said, "There was brilliant sunshine and all the church bells called the people together. They were dressed up and with their prayer books under their arms they went to church to listen to the minister."

11

There was enough gossip current to feed the imagination of these dutiful churchgoers. Vehement church controversies were going on; rumors had it that Kierkegaard had to finance his own publications; and, last but not least, there was also a tragic love affair that had ended in a broken engagement. There could be no doubt that this strange character, Sören Kierkegaard, was beyond the pale. The fate of the unrecognized genius was his to the bitter end. Shortly before he died, he wrote prophetically and with very good reason, "One thing I have come to know thoroughly: the abysmal lack of character in man. But how sad it is, there was yet some truth in me. And after my death they will all praise me in such a manner that the young people will believe I had been respected and revered in life. This, too, is part of the metamorphosis that truth suffers . . . in reality. The same contemporaries who have acted despicably will use the moment after death to say the contrary of yesterday, and thus everything will be confused."

Chapter 2

OUTWARD CONFUSION AND prophetic clarity were, indeed, the setting for Kierkegaard's entire life.

Sören Kierkegaard (1813–1855) was the youngest child of a large family. His father, Pedersen Michael Kierkegaard, was fifty-six when Sören was born, and his mother, forty-five. The father was a prosperous merchant, and the atmosphere of the home was one of comfort, strictest devotion to church and religion, and melancholy gloom. Michael Kierkegaard had grown up among the poor peasants of the Jütland heath. There, Moravian preachers had so deeply stirred up the people by a religious revival that even children labored under a sense of sin and wished they had never been born. Week after week thunderous sermons of damnation had been showering upon the peasants to shock them into virtue and frighten them into heaven.

The vocabulary of these dark hours had engraved itself deeply upon the mind of young Michael. It is no wonder that after learning of the "sacred wounds and holy blood," "hell being paved with the foreheads of sinful parsons," and youth "being the children of Satan himself," that one day when he was herding the sheep, Michael cursed this terrible God of wrath who would allow no sunshine and joy in his young life. This curse spread an even greater darkness over his life; he never forgave himself such blasphemy, and there was scarcely a smile on his face from that moment until his death at the age of eighty-two.

Young Sören was present at the interminable discussions his father held with his neighbors. Father Michael was not only a successful business man but also an intelligent reader of theological books. His stern methods of education kept the children indoors. Sören underwent the first exercises for his fertile imagination in extensive indoor "excursions" in the living room, where father and son marched up and down acting as though they were meeting acquaintances in the street, describing fictitious houses, trees, and people, lowering their voices as if the rattle of passing carriages had drowned them out, or commenting upon the produce of an imagined fruit market. The world of sin and guilt was of such reality to Sören that he wrote later, "I have been from childhood on in the grip of an overpowering melancholy . . . my sole joy being, as far as I can remember, that nobody could discover how unhappy I felt myself to be. . . . I have never really been a man, even less a child or youth."

Several times his father took him to the sermons of the famous Bishop Mynster. There was no doubt that the salvation of his soul was the most important concern in Sören's thinking and conversation, as the purity of his soul became his most serious endeavor in later life. For years his father's memory was fused with God's own image, and the old man's later confession of sexual excesses, the "great earthquake" (1835), not only shocked Sören out of reverence for his earthly father but also disrupted his devotion to his divine Father. He was deeply ashamed of his father, whom he thought he must henceforth approach "backward with his face turned away so as not to see his disgrace," just as Noah's sons had approached their drunken and naked father.

The curse of sin seemed to hang over the old man and his family: only the oldest son, Peder Christian, and Sören, the youngest of his children, survived. Michael's wife, Sören's mother, had been his servant before she became his second wife, and she remained a somewhat impersonal, shadowlike figure, about whom Sören remained almost entirely silent.

As a university student Sören devoted himself at first to theology but soon turned to the study of literature and philosophy. He lived the life of a bohemian intellectual, and in the style of his contemporaries extolled man's wit and reasoning power as the most fitting weapons for life. Since he had no financial worries, life did not seem bad, after all, and young Sören did not mind accumulating a rather considerable debt which his father had to pay.

The great change came when he broke his engagement to Regine Olsen, his attractive and lovely fiancée, who "was as light as a bird and as bold as a thought. . . ." He had met her when she was only fifteen, and after a two years' engagement, in 1841, he sent the engagement ring back to the disconsolate Regine with the following words: "In the Orient it means death to receive a silken cord, but in this case to mail the ring is likely to mean death for the sender." There were many mysteries about this step. Because he had missed the warmth of motherly love, did he need the virgin-mother image of this queen (*regina*), whom he continued to adore? Was celibacy one of the indispensable vows for his unordained ministry, itself a rejection of Luther's abolition of it? Did he consider Regine too light-hearted and happy a woman, incapable of bearing his melancholy? Might it have been that his poetic soul could no longer face reality and join *eros* and *agape* in matrimony? Was marriage too convenient a middle-class solution? The fact that he had loved Regine Olsen from the first day on as a poetic reflection of his memory and a lovely mirage rather than as a real being, may have rendered him incapable of marriage, as one of his analysts suspects, although Sören thought himself erotic to an extraordinary degree. Was a sexual sin of earlier years his "thorn in the flesh," of which he spoke repeatedly? Or was the breaking of his engagement perhaps one of his "acts of vengeance" upon society and himself, of which he liked to write? He whose conscience made him feel always in the wrong before God may have acted wrongly even toward his fiancée. He never ceased to love her, and her subsequent engagement and marriage to Fritz Schlegel caused him severe depression.

We have many answers to these questions, but the psychoanalysts, historians, and students of human nature seem unable to unveil the mystery of Sören Kierkegaard's private life. Even he himself, while taking great pains to let the mystery remain what it was, seemed puzzled, and the safest conclusion may be that the life of the spirit was to him the all-dominating concern to which everything else must be sacrificed. He felt called upon to do the "extraordinary thing" but as a writer and Christian, his inability to follow his heart's longing added to the painful memories of this penitent sinner.

This tragic interlude, which had followed by three years his sudden awakening to God's nearness in an experience of "indescribable joy" (1838), his pin-point existence as a solitary seeker after truth, the many open or veiled confessions in his writings, and the tragedy of having to endure the hostility of the public will always be fertile ground for the exploration of biographers and psychologists. The mystery of his genius may remain impenetrable to others; his destiny was equally inexplicable to himself.

In his diaries he calls himself a Janus whose one face laughs while the other one weeps. As a young man of twenty-five he wrote, "I too have both the tragic and the comic in me: I am witty and the people laugh—but I cry." A year earlier, his diary had spoken of practicing "vengeance upon the world" by acting gaily and consoling others but hiding his own anxiety, hoping that "if I can continue with this to my last day in life, I shall have had my revenge." He experienced, indeed, an oceanic feeling of anxiety which modern depth psychology calls a sense of unrelieved suspense. An entry in his diary, dated 1839, reads, "When I am alone in my kayak like a Greenlander, on the world's immense ocean, as much above the waters as underneath and always in God's hands, then it does occur to me to harpoon a sea monster on some good occasion . . . but I don't have the skill to do so." He was no Captain Ahab to attack Moby Dick, the white whale representing evil. His spiritual abode was the same melancholy that had haunted his father: "What the English say of their home, I have to say about my sadness; my sadness is my castle" (1839).

Chapter 3

RECENT STUDIES HAVE attempted to make a great deal of Kierkegaard's physical deformity as a hunchback. Rikard Magnussen has devoted two volumes to the mystery of Kierkegaard's appearance, concluding from his findings that his hunchback was that same "thorn in the flesh" of which Kierkegaard speaks so eloquently and which has given rise to so many other speculations. Theodor Haecker, the German Catholic expert on Kierkegaard, based a recent and rather verbose study on these "findings," exploiting them metaphysically as a God-given cross to be borne by the Danish writer. We wonder. Apparently Kierkegaard was of the pycnic type, and the effect of a hunchback upon his mind would lend a piquant touch to his psychological profile. But it is hard to see why his contemporary enemies should have been as discreet about the hunchback as they have been (apart from a suggestive cartoon or two) and why unhappy Regine Olsen continued to love him as ardently as ever after the breaking of the engagement. He was weak and sickly and he is likely to have derived from his physical impairment the same spirit of bravado that distinguished Dostoevsky and Nietzsche. But whatever the truth about the hunchback may be, it seems safe to remain conservative toward any of its psychological and religious interpretations.

The psychological impression which the various drawings of Kierkegaard's face convey range from the physiognomy of a pleasant and thoughtful poet to a withdrawn scholar. P. C. Klaestrup's sketch of the nineteen-year-old Sören is the most startling. Kierkegaard's wide and hypnotic eyes, the serious mouth, and high forehead combine to transmit some of the fervor of his passionate thoughts. We may never know which of these drawings is the most authentic.

There are more mysteries about his "thorn in the flesh." Can we consider his short story dealing with the anguish of a lonely bachelor, who considers it a possibility that he is the father of an illegitimate child, an autobiographical reference to his first and only contact with prostitution? If so, it might make another most interesting parallel to Nietzsche's experience in Cologne. Was the unrelieved self-reproach of the story's sad hero this same "thorn in the flesh"? No Freudian alibis were on hand a century ago, and the almost unbearable burden of Protestant sin theology would have been enough to crush Kierkegaard, the sensitive and overscrupulous seeker after purity of heart. Could it have been that such an incident—if at all true— reconciled him first to the confessions of his father and then to his divine Father? We may never know the truth. The mystery of genius ought rather to prevent our attaching too much importance to the incidents of his life and to the details of his appearance. Any attempt to interpret the mission and message of a genius like Kierkegaard through his biography is bound to remain inadequate. His religious message is universal, and the ways of the spirit are beyond and above the categories of psychology.

Chapter 4

IT WAS BOTH the burden and pride of Kierkegaard to be a writer, and the many facets of his strange personality expressed themselves brilliantly in his work. He spoke as a poet and scholar, seducer and moralist; he was joyful and witty but also desperately sad; a passionate fighter and a detached observer of others and himself, he was nothing to the exclusion of anything else. Like the possessed man in the parable of the Gadarene swine, he was "many" during the first phase of his writing, and it is one more of his life's mysteries that these almost unbearable tensions did not explode in the complete disorder of mental derangement.

This uncanny versatility of his genius expressed itself in the scintillating varieties of his style. Each time it is perfectly adapted to the overtones it wishes to convey. When he makes the seducer speak, his vocabulary is glib and persuasive; the faithful husband's words are clear and firm; the somber tone of his melancholy spreads a note of gloom; his religious ecstasies are truly infectious; his elegant humor is of the most facile kind; his vitriolic attacks upon church and clergy rally the reader to intense partisanship; and his sermons speak even to modern man's condition with the pathos of Biblical authority. And finally, when he wants to be nothing but the skeptical critic, he conveys an air of superiority that is convincing because it rises not from doubt but from a newly won and profound faith.

Kierkegaard was conscious of these contradictions within himself, knowing that between his melancholia and his true self there was "a world of fantasy which, in part, I have expressed through my pseudonyms." When publishing his *Papers of One Still Living* (1838), he added the remark that they were "published contrary to his will by S.K.," a note symbolic of his inward conflict. His writings during the first two stages of his life, the aesthetic and the ethical, appeared under suggestive, contradictory, and ultimately mysterious pen names, such as Victor Eremitus, Johannes de Silentio, Constantin Constantius, Johannes Climacus, Anti-Climacus, Frater Taciturnus, Inter and Inter, and Hilarius Bogbinder. The indirect method of conveying his thoughts by shreds of witticisms, anecdotes, and volcanic epigrams expressed itself in this disguise not only to camouflage his real personality—if one can speak of such an ultimate core of his being at all—but also to detach his thoughts from their author's personality; he was giving new laws for universal thinking and living.

Even his later works treat the religious with artful perfection and give his art everywhere a religious note. He who is initiated into such an overpowering vision of man's existence in the presence of God as Kierkegaard had been chosen to endure, sees no contradiction in such a method of communication. The universality of truth everywhere shines through; it is too enormous to be confined to any one style, and Kierkegaard, like Pascal two hundred years earlier and Nietzsche fifty years later, employs this method of indirect communication on the highest level. It was more than accidental that his doctor's thesis dealt with *The Concept of Irony,* this being perhaps the keenest medium for conveying truth by indirect suggestion.

The personal, or, as he preferred to call it, the subjective, thinker in Kierkegaard chose to speak thus in a highly controversial manner. In so doing he adapted himself perfectly to the nature of all spirituality, which is always a matter of experience and cannot be caught in the images of logical communication. The more concrete and positive we are in speaking about God, the lower is the level of comprehending Him, as Kierkegaard illustrated in his *Religious Discourses* and *Exercise in Christianity.* Religion resides in the interior and spiritual realm and eludes logical or direct communication. Jesus' fondness for teaching in parables, a method open to many interpretations, is related to this fact. As we shall see in a later chapter, Kierkegaard never tired of stressing the nature of existence as becoming, fluctuating, evolving, and its logical formulation is always apt to be inauthentic (Heidegger), too massive, and stationary. Moreover, the essence of human existence is uncertainty, the very realm in which faith (not knowledge) must live to become meaningful. Thus indirect suggestion toward truth is the only adequate vehicle for its mysterious character. Even in the realm of ordinary human sympathy, pity, or hate, our most adequate expressions are indirect and symbolical, as, incidentally, modern psychoanalysis has verified, not only for our dream life but for the whole domain of subconscious or involuntary suggestions.

Indirect communication in the realm of religious truth necessitates the making of moral choices. It involves also a hidden appeal to the listener to explore his own situation for insufficiency and guilt, and to view earnestly his potential future. Its most mysterious expression concerns the fact that God, unlimited and eternal, cannot be comprehended by man's ordinary logical processes. Christ, claiming to be God and man, is the absolute paradox; he is eternal truth coming into being in time; he lived 1900 years ago but is contemporaneous with the believer; he is a "sign of contradiction" as are his parables and miracles, and, finally, he is as much an offense to our logic as he was unacceptable to his contemporaries. Belief alone can comprehend the paradox, an attitude that will risk an experiment in living. Dostoevsky's Staretz Zossima meant this same existential faith when he told the doubting woman that she would become convinced of God's reality to the degree that she progressed in practicing Christian love. Christian faith is something to be lived; it cannot be comprehended *in abstracto*.

Chapter 5

KIERKEGAARD'S WAY OF expressing his convictions in word and deed affected to the breaking point his relationship with Bishop Mynster, Professor Nielsen, and his own brother. Much of what he said and wrote was open to misinterpretation, although he abandoned his method of indirect communication in his final years when launching his attack upon the Church. Copenhagen pilloried him "with deadly grins." It is likely that his final and undisguised attacks upon "official Christianity" remained incomprehensible to the average church member of his day, but the higher clergy must have sensed how irrefutable and prophetic his writings were. He shared with the later Nietzsche the fate of many a genius in remaining unrecognized for too long a time in his own country, and—partly on account of the little-known Danish language—in all Europe and America. "The lull and deadness of order," of which Dostoevsky speaks with much less justification than Kierkegaard, was a heavy mist hanging over the spiritual and intellectual sky of Denmark. The country's obtuseness to basic religious thinking was likewise affected by political events in the 1840's.

Sören Kierkegaard directed these religious attacks against his father's confessor, Bishop Mynster, who had confirmed him at the age of fifteen and whose administrative skill and polished oratory had retrieved many of Denmark's leading citizens for an active share in church life. Kierkegaard considered Mynster the symbol of Christianity's compromise with the state and with worldly interests. The state, so Kierkegaard maintained, dominated the church, whereas the church should have shaken its members out of the middle-class complacency that made them "listen with their hands folded over the stomach, directing a sleepy look upward." Mynster, the government-appointed church president, was to Kierkegaard an enemy of Christ's teachings. According to Kierkegaard, there never could be a reconciliation between the world and the demands of Christ; the two were poles apart. If Christ were to come again, he would encounter the same hostility as of old. A generation before Dostoevsky wrote his classical scene between the unbelieving Grand Inquisitor and the returned Christ, Kierkegaard had already envisioned some of the essence of this remarkable Russian legend. Mynster was to him a gentle but nonetheless dangerous forbear of the demonic Grand Inquisitor; he and his clerical subordinates had made a successful career by preaching Christ's prophecy that His followers would be persecuted. The very foundation of Christianity in Denmark and all Europe rested not on spiritual strength but on the political power and financial resources of the state. To be a Christian, in Kierkegaard's opinion, could mean only to be persecuted, to be a "Single One" before God and lonely among men. Now that everyone had become a nominal Christian, Christianity had ceased to exist. The church was a travesty of Christianity.

Sören Kierkegaard centered his attack on this state of affairs upon Bishop Mynster, whom he made the symbol of a complacent and well established Lutheran Church. Actually the Bishop, while rather unoriginal in his thinking, was a well meaning and unambitious man. A similar and even more painful conflict arose between Sören and his brother, Peder Christian, Bishop of Aalborg, a quieter and less conspicuous figure than Mynster. In defending himself, Peder went so far as to publish during these controversies a lecture against Sören, characterizing him as unrealistic, ecstatic, and eccentric. His one remaining confidant was Professor Nielsen, but Sören was soon to discover that the respected scholar exploited many of his privately expressed thoughts in his own philosophical publications. Sören realized then that he was to remain forever a lonely prophet in the wilderness, truly a Single One before God. His road was the *via solitaria*.

From that time on (1846), he confided his intimate

thoughts only to his various journals. He had reached the final stage of solitude and was now confronted only by God. Kierkegaard wanted no pity, though he had hoped to have a fair hearing for his message. Like Nietzsche he wanted no disciples, "the greatest of all misfortunes"; yet to find himself almost without sympathizers was a bitter Gethsemane experience. He could not forget Regine Olsen and his broken engagement; indeed, he owed her memory such profound insight into man's relationship with God that the somewhat over-enthusiastic Russian philosopher Shestov, studying Kierkegaard in his later life, declared that Regine Olsen was more important than the discovery of America. Repeatedly Kierkegaard likened the individual's relationship with God to a lover's experience. It is at once painful and happy, passionate but unfulfilled, lived in time yet infinite. Once he had separated himself from Regine Olsen he was free to enter upon his "engagement to God."

Toward the end of his short life in a series of vehemently worded leaflets known as *The Moment,* or *The Instant,* he extended his criticism of Danish conditions to an attack upon all Christendom. The leaflets were primarily directed against Professor Martensen, who had publicly spoken of the deceased Bishop Mynster as a Witness of Truth. Kierkegaard was incensed by the use of the term "witness" (meaning "martyr" in the Greek original) for a highly paid career minister. The "little word" rallied every vestige of his waning energy for the writing of those indignant pages which have become classic in their power to arouse a Christian conscience.

Chapter 6

THE ESTABLISHED OR state church of Denmark was the Lutheran Church. The nation considered it a God-given duty to protect the Church, to promote its welfare by instituting compulsory religious training in all schools, and to safeguard the clergy by assuring them a respectable economic level and by giving them the status of civil servants.

It was against this system of security and state control that Kierkegaard rebelled. The security of a Christian Church meant to him the betrayal of every tenet of Christ's teaching and example. To live "Christianly" should be identical with shouldering the greatest possible insecurity before man and God. Christ's disciples suffered persecution and death; they had no official status and were never recognized in any manner or form. The anonymous early Christian followers were martyred, not honored, paid, and respected for belonging to the Church. "Beware of the scribes, who like to go about in long robes, and love salutations in the market places and the best seats in the synagogues and the places of honor at feasts" (Luke 20:46). Originally, to become a follower of Christ had meant not so much as a "hole like the foxes" for sleep, or a "nest like the birds of heaven" for security. Nowadays, so wrote Kierkegaard, the young minister becomes a "seeker" after having finished his theological training. But he is not a seeker after the Absolute; he seeks a clerical position. In this he is basically different from Socrates, who received no salary for teaching youth, and Christ, who was the friend of the poor.

Kierkegaard's personal decision to refuse a Church appointment was, therefore, a logical step, especially after the Church authorities and the public had shown signs of being alarmed by his books *The Sickness Unto Death* and *Exercise in Christianity*. The following ironical dialogue from *The Instant* illustrates his uncompromising position in this regard: "Did the apostle Paul have an official position?"—"No, Paul had no official position."—"Did he make much money by some other means?"—"No, he did not make much money at all."—"Wasn't he then at least married?"—"No, Paul was not married."—"But Paul, then, was not at all a serious man!"—"No, Paul was not a serious man."

Kierkegaard did not pass up any opportunity for taking his revenge on life in a manner that was less mysterious than at times he made it appear. Here is one more of his stories which served his untiring campaign against the clergy: A Swedish parson who was deeply touched by the impression his sermon had made upon his flock tried to calm his congregation by remarking, "Don't cry, my children. There is still a chance that it is not all true." Why, asks Kierkegaard, does the minister of today not say this any longer? The answer is that it is no longer necessary; we all know it—now that all of us are of the universal priesthood.

Christianity's tragedy, then, is that it is no longer what it was meant to represent, a militant, suffering, protesting minority. Since all of us have become Christians, the essence of Christ's teachings has become watered down to such a thin trickle of public morality, a sort of police ordinance, that we have succeeded in abolishing Christianity in the name of Christianity. "Why do we no longer see the contradiction between Christianity's nature as polemical and the state's essence as a quantitative entity? Why don't we see how the state is paying its officers to destroy Christianity. . . ?" Such was Kierkegaard's anguish in 1854, one year before his death, and thirty years before Tolstoy's volcanic voice levelled similar accusations against the Russian Orthodox Church.

Chapter 7

KIERKEGAARD HAD SPIRITUAL ancestors in this opposition to official Christianity and the clergy. Almost two hundred years earlier, the first Quaker, George Fox, had risen in England with a vigorous testimony against the "hireling priests" of his age and had tried to restore "primitive Christianity," to use William Penn's words, in the layman's church, such as Quakerism in its strongest groups has remained ever since. Tersteegen's pietism in Germany had injected a considerable element of this spiritual democracy into the bloodstream of Protestantism, but Kierkegaard took up his fight single-handed and with no claims to historic continuity. He was quite aware of his extraordinary task, solemnly stating that the reformers before him had done everything "for the expansion of Christianity," whereas he was to arrest this expansion and internalize faith. He knew that the Christianity he demanded was austere and uncompromising. He hoped that Bishop Mynster would express at least some sympathy with his ideas, but Mynster had remained aloof.

These attacks upon the established Church represented for the most part the negative aspect of Kierkegaard's labors, an approach that was to become a much more dangerous weapon in the hands of later social revolutionaries like Karl Marx, men who numbered the Church among the forces used by the possessing classes to keep the proletariat docile and subdued. Kierkegaard's attacks make no references to social conditions or to scientific progress which was later to become another source of religious malcontents. He was a conservative in politics and theology. His private war was dictated exclusively by his sense of religious honesty. He felt divinely elected to fulfill a most disagreeable but necessary task, apostolic in its mission, but shocking to his fellow Christians. The appalling charges of corruption hurled unconditionally against all ministers was undoubtedly unjust, and his words of farewell and love on his deathbed may have been another of his veiled confessions of wrongdoing. He never tired of thanking God for His grace and for the strength he owed Him. Worship and prayer were his daily practice, as doubt was his daily companion. At the end, great inward clarity and peace came over him.

Chapter 8

IN SEPTEMBER, 1855, he collapsed in the street, like Nietzsche; refused to take the last sacraments at the hands of a "state official"; and asked only to be remembered to all the people whom he had loved but who had never been able to understand his sufferings.

One of his Danish biographers, O. P. Monrad, epitomized his whole life as an unhappy lover and unsuccessful writer into the flippant sentence, "A story of an engagement, a little ink of a satirical paper, a little word in a speech—that is all." When Monrad wrote this in 1909, he could not know that Kierkegaard's thinking was to incite the minds of theologians and philosophers to even more passionate controversies than he had ever hoped to raise in his own time.

Chapter 9

IN 1840, ALMOST one hundred years before it became an historic fact, Kierkegaard had prophesied nothing less than the "total bankruptcy toward which the whole of Europe seems to be heading." He spoke at a time when the European masses had not yet projected their problems into every phase of life by sheer weight of numbers and by their many claims. Yet even during his lifetime he sensed that the day was approaching when a personal religious message would fall on deaf ears. "Ultimately," he wrote, "it is the masses at whom I have directed my polemics . . ." but the "believers" did not care to listen. "So little do the people understand me that they will not even understand my complaint that they do not understand me." He had considered it his task to "revise the vocation of a Christian," and "they all, even Bishop Mynster, know that I am right. . . ." As was the case with Dostoevsky and Nietzsche, his periods of pride at times approached arrogance; but his humility more frequently gave way to despair.

A few months before his death he wrote, "This is the road we all have to travel . . . over the bridge of sighs to eternity." A prolific writer who had produced his work at a torrential speed, he had not succeeded in remaining incognito as he had intended. He had started his career in 1838, at the age of twenty-five, by attacking Hans Christian Andersen, the poet of fairy tales; he ended by accusing Christianity openly of corruption and of "Christian crime." But Denmark continued to prefer Hans Christian Andersen's brilliant sunshine over life, the lyrical sound of church bells, Sunday clothes, and a not too disturbing sermon by the minister, to Kierkegaard's inconvenient message. And for too long a time the Paris of the North went on regarding him as an eccentric who well deserved to be the butt of street urchins and of gossiping towns-people.

Chapter 10

THE FINAL PHASE of Kierkegaard's existence was the last of the three stages of evolving spiritual life which he, like any other religious man, experienced: the aesthetic, the ethical, and the religious stages (*Either-Or*). There is no doubt but that Kierkegaard retained, for the greater part of his life at least, some of the aesthete's, or more precisely, the poet's traits; for example, he loved sarcasm and continued to the very last to use sardonic irony. But he considered a reconciliation of these three stages impossible: the life of the spirit moves upward in abrupt stages of growth.

These stages have in our time assumed an added interest because of the claims of modern existentialism, which regards Kierkegaard as its progenitor. Yet there is little genuine spiritual relationship between Kierkegaard and the most conspicuous of the French existentialists, Sartre and Camus. Their thinking remains largely within the limits of the first of these stages, the aesthetic.

In the aesthetic stage man cultivates the mood of an enjoyable but deceptive harmony or pleasure, of which Kierkegaard's own *Diary of the Seducer* and the masterful analysis of Mozart's *Don Juan* are outstanding examples. Man detaching himself from moral struggle and indulging in the search for beauty and pleasure remains within the realm of unreality and dream. Everything becomes play, passive enjoyment, or poetic delusion. History assumes the shadowlike contours of a myth, while reality loses its true character. The aesthete constructs for himself a fictitious world of dreams, lives only in the immediate present, and finds himself ultimately rejected by life's moral realities, as Nietzsche's later tragedy illustrates. It is a dead-end route that leads to boredom and disgust and deprives life of all meaning. The aesthete possesses only the present moment; he is self-centered and despairing,

31

searching for more pleasures to escape from this despair, only to learn that his evasion of moral and religious reality leads him into nothingness. Like young Parsifal, he does not know how to ask the right questions about the meaning of suffering and life. He never asks whether he is guilty, and he resembles Doctor Faustus by living in an abysmal vacuum. Kierkegaard applies his condemnation of pure thinking, as treason to the spirit, with equal vigor to the poet when he says: "From the Christian point of view and in spite of all aesthetics, any poet's existence is a sin, viz., the sin that one is writing poetry instead of living; that one occupies oneself with God and truth only in one's imagination instead of aiming at experiencing both existentially" (*Either-Or; The Sickness Unto Death*).

Much of Kierkegaard's condemnation pertains prophetically to Nietzsche's later praise of life as "an aesthetic phenomenon" which to him was the only value which justified it. Nietzsche did not recognize Christian ethics or a moral world principle; his final despair and his contourless vision of a new life support Kierkegaard's warning expressed a generation earlier.

Such is also the mood of the existentialism of which Sartre and Camus are the exponents. Sartre illustrates the artist's despair graphically in his novel *Nausea* and Camus in his essay on Sisyphus, who realizes the futility of his existence but persists nevertheless with a sort of melancholy courage in trying to give some meaning to his life. Some existentialists seem, however, far from feeling, in this nothingness, a sensation of being lost. They praise it as a delirious sense of freedom, a new reality devoid of the theories, beliefs, traditions, and clichés which camouflaged our former ignorance and insecurity. Their new world has, to be sure, neither security nor authority, but it awaits man's new decisions—of some vague kind.

Sartre praises this freedom as Promethean. His play, *The Flies,* dramatizes the Greek legend of Orestes, who murders his mother Clytemnestra and her husband Aegisthes. Orestes, rising above any fear of divine punishment, shouts at Jupiter, "I am neither master nor slave, I am my own freedom! Hardly hadst thou created me when I already ceased to be thy own!" The qualms of conscience are, therefore, no longer the reminders of moral laws. They are nothing more than bothersome flies, an insect pest that man must fight off in order to maintain his independence. Man, according to Sartre, is seldom aware of his freedom. "It hits him," as in the case of Orestes, "like lightning." The gods have lost all power over him, and he affirms happily Nietzsche's proclamation that "God has died." Repentance would merely cancel out any freedom, a freedom which "chases the gods from their ancient thrones." Man must "invent his own way."

Sartre calls this quite arbitrarily the "new humanism," centered on man in contrast to a God-centered way of life. Such a use of the term "humanism" is arbitrary because humanism has never believed in an unbridled yielding to instincts and complete detachment from the laws of morality. It believes in the freedom of the individual for the sake of his own moral perfection and that of society. Sartre's freedom is nothing but moral anarchy. He is unhappy because he is, as it were, sentenced to be free. Sartre recognizes only these categories of human existence: accident, necessity, liberty, aloneness, and senselessness. The old faith, that man has a destiny prescribed by a higher authority, is gone; he is now "free." But this freedom results in moral alienation from his fellow man and the subsequent fear of life, or pan-anxiety. We must choose what to do but will never know whether our choice was the right one. One can never define a man as long as he lives because "he is his life and nothing else." Life then has no pattern or providential design; it is meaningless, and despair is, therefore, only logical. Such a philosophy is a far cry from Kierkegaard's remark in his *Journal* that "life must be understood backwards but it must be lived forwards."

Camus, too, believes that life is senseless, but he still endeavors to find a meaning for it. His insoluble dilemma is to see a chance for moral perfection without believing in

God. He asks, "Is it possible to become a saint without believing in God? That is the sole concrete problem worth considering nowadays." In his play *Caligula* he recognizes an obligation toward his fellow man without being able to solve the inherent moral problem, but at least his effort in the direction of moral perfection moves him closer to a genuine humanism than Sartre ever has been or may be in the future. Like Sartre, who has promised to write a code of ethics at some future date, Camus leaves us without moral guidance.

Chapter 11

SUCH IS THE world beyond good and evil in which Nietzsche and many of Dostoevsky's characters are prominent citizens. To Kierkegaard the French existentialists or Heidegger's atheistic philosophy would never have been more than the excessive and ultimate consequences of the aesthetic, or contemplative, stage in life, a stage which he did not consider part of true existence. The only traits shared in common between the French and German existentialists and a religiously conceived existentialism are the intense awareness of life's darkness and a sense of suspense resulting in that all-pervading anxiety, or fear, of all life which Kafka has dramatized so convincingly. The religious existentialists of our time (Nicholas Berdyaev, Gabriel Marcel, and perhaps Karl Jaspers) recognize the claims of God, or the Absolute, upon man, while realizing that man is acting largely in the dark when he attempts to serve God's will. But in this darkness man is touching the seam of God's garment, and he will not end in despair. He has faith in God's ultimate victory.

Thus, as far as Sartre and his friends are concerned, the choice of their name as existentialists is arbitrary and misleading. Kierkegaard limits the term "existence"—he never spoke of existentialism—to the ethical and religious level. "To exist as a human being means to exist ethically" (*Postscript*) and to face perpetually new moral choices. Aesthetic man remains detached and static, but ethical man is in the process of becoming. He evolves as a personality which combines the universal with his subjective being and thus partakes of eternity. In this stage man may achieve stability and authentic leadership and assume an affirmative attitude toward life. This makes the true beauty of life, which aesthetic man fails to discover in the multitude of things and relationships that present themselves in an attractive guise to him. Don Juan sought in vain the rich human soul in the many women he knew, but "marriage," so writes Kierkegaard, the celibate, "is the most important exploration which man can undertake."

Some of his views are likely to be rejected by modern Christians. The profundity of his religious insight is, nevertheless, unforgettable as, for example in the following passage: "Let man be man, and the woman be woman. Exactly then can a woman be everything to man. As a woman she understands the finite and therefore can give it to man. Without the woman man is a restless spirit finding no peace because he is nowhere at home. Why do the Scriptures not say that woman should leave father and mother and cleave unto man? Isn't she the weaker one to find refuge with man? But no, it says, the man shall leave father and mother and cleave unto his wife. And the Scriptures are right: she is stronger inasmuch as the wife gives man the finite; she is his refuge. I rejoice in understanding the importance of the woman that way; to me she thus becomes the symbol of the community. The spirit is in an embarrassing situation if it cannot dwell within a community and therefore not impart itself in it. For the community which the spirit needs to find a home in the finite world, there is indeed no more beautiful symbol than a wife."

A writer of inimitable skill and flexibility, Kierkegaard could not fail to consider his own favorite media of expression, irony, and humor. Irony functions somewhere between the aesthetic and the moral. Born of dissatisfaction and coldly critical of any imperfection, it remains egotistical and does not invite consent in spite of its possible truthfulness. But humor reveals understanding. It has a warm, forgiving, and sympathetic note and reconciles us with weakness or sin, whereas irony remains haughty and critical. There is, then, in humor the suggestion of a religious conscience, a sense of tragedy combined with the comic, and a promise of hope or reconciliation. But it may also contain a note of loneliness and even pain; it is frequently beyond communication and born from suffering; it thus prepares the religious stage in life.

Chapter 12

SINCE EXISTENCE MEANS the making of moral choices, it is a perpetual *Either-Or* and a life of action. As a synthesis of the infinite and the finite, the eternal and the temporal, man's dilemma is to have to meet decisions in the uncharted realm of moral living. Existence is emphatically not a new system of philosophy, or a new view taken of life. Man's intelligence can never remain outside the totality of life and look upon it as a spectator may look at something outside himself. "Pure thinking," says Kierkegaard, "is a phantom." Man who merely contemplates a truth is apt to become a "traitor like Judas." In our time Julien Benda has raised the equally severe reproach against the intellectuals that they have committed treason against those whom they were meant to lead, by living in an ivory tower of self-sufficiency (*La Trahison des Clercs*). Pure thinking overlooks the creative processes of God, to whom the term "existence" is not applicable. According to Kierkegaard, "God does not think, He creates; God does not exist; He is eternal."

Man's only adequate approach to life is faith-knowledge and not the much vaunted objective reasoning of the philosopher who erects a majestic palace of logical thinking in his systems but continues to live in a dog house. Reason is bound to the questions, "For what and why am I doing this or that?" or, "For what and why is this happening?" But God's work is beyond the limits of understanding, and He may appear as unreasonable to us as His demand of Abraham that he kill his son Isaac. Yet He is wise in a mysterious manner although appearing paradoxical to us. Any truth is a *complexio oppositorum,* to use Jakob Boehme's term, a "troubled truth," leading to despair as long as faith does not give it direction.

It is obvious that this existential emphasis is not meant to be a new system of thought like Hegel's philosophy, against which Kierkegaard rose as passionately as he attacked all philosophy based on reason alone. It is, of course, possible to construct a logical system which pretends to include all aspects of life, a catalogue of that which is, but logic is itself part of God's creation and cannot step outside itself to appraise the totality of life. It must transcend itself in faith. The philosophical existentialist inverts Descartes' "I think, therefore I am" by stating, "I am, therefore I think." But the religious existentialist will have to say, "I believe, therefore I am."

It seems important to stress that Kierkegaard did not radically negate logical or rational thinking, a realm in which he was himself a master. Rather he emphasized the idea that while we live in the realm of thinking, it must be thinking that commits us and becomes congruent with living.

There are, again, paradoxes, or seeming contradictions, in this existential demand: to move toward the light requires a leap into the dark; singleness of purpose is needed to reach totality; only the simple mind will grasp the complex; the subjective, or personal, leads to unity with the objective; the eternal is experienced in time. The existential bestows an authentic character upon the I; the self is not dissolved as in mysticism, pantheism, or religious romanticism. It is, nevertheless, in danger of regarding that in the self as authentic which is unauthentic, arbitrary, or irrelevant.

When Kierkegaard declares that man's existence is an experience or a process of sustained becoming (developing), he is, of course, not thinking of psychological or biological growth. Man evolves, or becomes, by moral striving and tension. He can, therefore, never *be* a Christian but only attempt to *become* one. Suffering, to which he, like Dostoevsky, gives paramount importance, is the element "in which that which is religious begins to breathe"; suffering is, therefore, "the beginning." Part of this suffering is man's consciousness of guilt, which cries out for his reconciliation with God. And since man is the meeting ground for God's eternal demands, he will have many clashes with the world. But the process of becoming is primarily an inward growth and must be fired by the passionate desire, feeling, and imagination which are so deplorably absent in Christianity.

Kierkegaard never tires of emphasizing this passionate character of the seeker in a manner almost identical with that used by the later Nietzsche. But Kierkegaard also discloses a new paradox in this passionate search: man must not assert himself. To grow before God means to become small, to be like children, or even to be despised and persecuted, an experience that was vividly present in Kierkegaard's own short life. And man, believing he has found God, will at once sense his distance from Him because he realizes that in the face of God he is a sinner.

Chapter 13

THE CRISIS EXPERIENCE begins when man faces the nothing and senses a fear or anxiety that is the beginning of despair (*Either-Or* and *The Concept of Dread*). Man must make the paradoxical "leap" into faith, from which he will receive an existential certitude in God. Kierkegaard launched his first powerful attacks against rationalism with such thoughts, which were seized by the existentialist school of thinking in our day as bases for its claim to being its spiritual successor.

Modern existentialism "covers a multitude of sins" (Alexander Dru) and ranges in its serious representatives from atheism (Heidegger, Sartre) to Protestant biblicism (Barth), Kantianism (Jaspers), Catholic social existentialism (Gabriel Marcel), and the neo-orthodoxy of Reinhold Niebuhr. In spite of some basic differences, their opposition to the primacy of reason is as impressive as their emphasis upon our crisis or frontier situation. All of them stress the pathos of existence as experienced in either an urelieved dread or the passionate desire to partake of God's infinity. All serious existential thinking has administered a severe blow to our intellectualism; and the new and unlimited perspectives given the universe by modern science have produced the view that "an infinite universe of indefinite limits has no definite place for a finite man," as Karl Löwith formulated man's predicament.

Kierkegaard would hardly have subscribed to this latter statement, as he could not have accepted the vague assertion that our crisis and dread are the essence or being of man (Heidegger, Sartre). The paradox of modern existentialism is that it has created new systems of thought in spite of its effort to persuade us that reason is an insufficient tool for shaping a world view. Kierkegaard insisted on transcendence into the realm of faith in a manner similar to Nietzsche's later emphasis upon the perpetual inward

contradiction in man, the tension between time and eternity, and the absurd or paradoxical
life. The direction of striving was
but Kierkegaard and Nietzsche co
for transcendence.

Kierkegaard's concern with the
ual's encounter with God was to
an all-absorbing passion. The Ch
and static institution for whose m
points one thousand approved (o
Christianity perishes in the ensui
anity of nincompoops" is nothing
marking the final decay of a Ch
to be a spiritually growing, or b
such also an *ecclesia militans*. K
experience in the actual Church
which he expected of a religious
Christ; according to him the t
found only in the Eternal, Invisi

We have seen how adamant
against whom he primarily d
Christendom. "One hears often
priests, that one cannot live on n
priests manage to do just that.
and yet they live on it." Such
writings. The term "Christian" was to him a polemical
term, so that "one can be a Christian only in opposition"
to the world or to other men. As soon as this contrast is
eliminated, the vocation of a Christian has lost its object.
"Such is the case in our 'Christianity' which has slyly abolished Christianity by saying 'we are all Christians.'"
Christianity has lost its vitality and is senile. We call anyone a Christian whose entire life belongs to other realms,
who never goes to Church, never thinks of God, and never
mentions His name "except when swearing." The state recognizes these people as Christians, "the Church buries
them as Christians, and they are dispatched to eternity as
Christians."

Similarly and with equal logic Kierkegaard applied his concept of becoming, or evolving and striving, to the individual Christian. The Christian will always be in the wrong before God, because "between God and man there is an infinite, yawning, qualitative difference," a statement identical with Karl Barth's modern emphasis on God's "otherness." Man is impotent, but God can achieve everything, even our turning to faith; so great is the grace inherent in the beginning of all Christianity in man.

Such austere demands upon the individual are diametrically opposed to most of our modern peace-of-mind thinking. Kierkegaard would never have exchanged the wisdom of Job for the techniques of psychological massage that promise such smooth sailing to those following Rabbi Liebman. The essential condition of this never-ending process of becoming a Christian, is, according to Kierkegaard, unrest, unpeace of mind, and insecurity—an internal motion to be borne only in prayer and repentance, during which the individual stands "before God" in solitude.

There has never been a reformed Church, and Kierkegaard, the Protestant, attacks the Reformation as critically as Nietzsche did a generation later from a different angle. Only the individual is to be reformed, as only the individual can undergo the conversion erroneously attributed to evangelistic movements as a whole. God, for Kierkegaard, is primarily the refuge of the sinner, and the sinner's salvation lies exclusively in maintaining his faith, a doctrine quite in keeping with Luther's justification by faith. He who realizes his state of sinfulness is *eo ipso* a Christian because he measures his morality (or rather his lack of it) by Christian standards. The unbeliever does not have the religious experience of remorse; he does not "exist" in the Kierkegaardian sense. Existence for the individual means at one and the same time closeness to God and conflict, unity and rupture, introspection and transcendence. The existing believer has a liberating sense of freedom because God's grace allows him to partake of eternity. He is not like Sartre's "free" man "condemned to be free," but ennobled to live in freedom as a daring quest.

The emphasis of some modern existentialists on dread, fear, anxiety, or "Angst" differs from Kierkegaard's concept of the corresponding term. His anxiety is moral and spiritual. Man's original state is one of innocence, as was that of Adam before his fall. But he has knowledge of guilt, or sin; and anxiety, or dread, in the presence of weakness is a permanent condition. The realm of moral and spiritual striving is never secure but of uncertain potentialities. Virtue includes an apprehension of this potential power of sin (or the nothing). For Heidegger this nothingness is an ontological condition whereas Kierkegaard (and, incidentally, also Freud) considers it a psychological state. The prohibition given to Adam not to eat from the forbidden tree produced in him this state of anxiety because he realized in the temptation the potential termination of his "eternity." It was sexuality that introduced the temporal into Adam's life. Existence, then, as a moral and spiritual state of suspense implies this "thorn in the flesh." Nearness to God can be experienced only in contrast to possible or actual alienation from Him. Only through extreme spiritual anguish can faith be won.

Existence, according to Kierkegaard, is, therefore, a state of anxious suspense for which Jesus' Gethsemane experience is the supreme example. Only the paradoxical "leap into faith" will give man certitude in God. The opposite of sin is not virtue but faith.

Chapter 14

THE IDEAL BELIEVER is of necessity solitary. His experience is secret, subjective, and yet in a mysterious sense also communal. In dwelling on this subject (*Religious Discourses, Concept of the Chosen Ones*), Kierkegaard adorns the image of this Single One with almost supernatural attributes and speaks of him in terms similar to those which Nietzsche employed later for the coming Superman. He says, "This spiritual man will rank as high above man as man is above the animal." He has not yet come; but since time and eternity are one in the sight of God, he is already present in a mysterious manner. He is an idea without limitations, and his *via eminentia* represents the most decisive Christian category. The Single One remains incognito and silent, alone before God, and unrecognizable by any external characteristic. As in Nietzsche's Superman, his silence and nobility are inseparable; he guards his thoughts and thus remains strong, residing in a realm where the masses can never be. His significance may become known only indirectly: he will be the world's victim.

Kierkegaard's emphasis upon the Single One illustrates once more his method of indirect communication, for which Socrates was his master. Socrates' skill in suggesting and finally liberating an eternally existing truth from the mind of the individual by his *maieutic* (mid-wifery of the intellect) method and his contribution to the disintegration of paganism are comparable to Kierkegaard's aim in proving that truth must rise from the existence of an individual instead of being merely equated with an intellectual insight. Kierkegaard, like Socrates, believed he was living in a period of decline; he felt that he had to "reintroduce Christianity into Christendom."

Eternal truth, present in the soul, must be "recollected forward" in the process of repetition and recurrence. Essentially, there is no division of time into past, present, and future; eternity is the absolute. When eternity enters man in the revelation of truth, Kierkegaard speaks of it as The Moment. The Moment is always a judgment experience, since man is made to see the temporal under the aspect of the eternal. The Single One achieves this. Much of Kierkegaard's concept of Repetition again suggests Nietzsche's "eternal recurrence," but Kierkegaard's Single One is distinguished from the Superman by his striving for humility in the sight of God, a quality which the Superman rejects.

Kierkegaard was aware of the religious contradiction implicit in the praise of such a detached aristocratic being, for he wrote, "If I conduct myself like others I shall be a betrayer; if I separate from them, I betray myself." As so often, his heart and mind are divided between the opposite poles of truth. Yet he adheres to the austere demands of his idea, with which most people have no *rapport*. As in the time of Christ the mass man joins a group because others have done so before him, and truth will achieve recognition because of the weight of supporting numbers, not because of its inherent character (*Journal*). Yet his *Attack upon Christendom* also praises the "plain man," whom he seems to distinguish from the better situated middle-class man. There is something of Dostoevsky's respect for the simple mind in his remark that "I have not separated my life from thine; thou knowest it. I have lived in the street and am known to all. Moreover, I have not achieved any importance . . . therefore, if I belong anywhere, I must belong to thee. . . ."

Nevertheless, Kierkegaard's emphasis on the Single One's exclusiveness is apt to give the impression that he, like Nietzsche, forgets the mission of this enlightened One who ought to set his soul to calling out of the crowd those forces which will bring about the Kingdom. The Single One should convey God's guidance to his companions. A full relationship with God implies a loving relationship with one's fellow man. It cannot afford to overlook the humility of which Kierkegaard speaks elsewhere so eloquently.

Chapter 15

KIERKEGAARD'S CRITICAL ATTITUDE toward the mass man refers, of course, to the educated middle-class, who antedated the proletarian mass man by almost half a century. Max Stirner's *The Single One and His Own* (1845) was the first angry voice in the growing chorus of those who were critical of the mass man. But Stirner's Single One was meant to be a revolutionary who was to fight the docility and indifference of the masses. Dostoevsky's Grand Inquisitor in *The Brothers Karamazov* (1880) expostulated with the returning Christ that freedom is too heavy a burden for the mass man to bear and that he is anxious to be relieved of his freedom and is ready to be guided like a child. Nietzsche's Zarathustra (1883) despised the masses, including the educated mass man, as the "much-too-many" over whom the Superman was to rise and rule. Gustave LeBon's prophetic study of the *Psychology of the Masses* (1895), translated as *The Crowd,* reads now like a modern document. Thirty years before the advent of European totalitarianism LeBon analyzed the fickle character of the mass man precisely as he has evolved under the rule of Mussolini, Hitler, and Stalin. Of Mussolini it was said that he knew this book by heart, but Hitler and Goebbels undoubtedly mastered its essence by the diabolic intuition of their malignant genius. Oswald Spengler's cold disdain for the masses in *The Decline of the West* (1918–1922) fills pages upon pages with the most cynical observations of the mass man's immaturities. And though José Ortega y Gasset's attitude is constructive and educational, his *Revolt of the Masses* (1930) is likewise burdened with dire apprehensions and sound observations on the unpredictable shallowness of the mass man's psychology.

Several of these writers concern themselves with political and social freedom, that paradoxical burden so hard to bear, yet the spiritual freedom to make moral and religious decisions, an even greater burden, must supply the energies for the desire to be free politically and socially. Kierkegaard ignored the scientific and social conditions of his time in his quest for the inner freedom. Though he lived and wrote when Karl Marx's *Communist Manifesto* (1848) was published, neither Marx's scientific socialism nor the French socialism of the 1830's seems to have made any impression upon his thinking.

If he were living today, he would in all likelihood center again upon the religious core of our confusion. The discussion of political and social freedom in our time has become almost entirely a matter of political philosophy and strategy. We are in danger of forgetting that our Christian heritage of spiritual freedom is the most productive source for our struggle in the realm of politics and social reform. A hundred years ago, Kierkegaard wrote that "Christianity in our times is close to becoming paganism; it has long ago yielded at least its main points." He was right and wrong in that strange duality in which much of his thinking moved.

The trend toward paganism, or secularism, has increased, but the conscious resistance of Christian forces is also gaining in momentum. We have seen that the Church as an organization lacked the strength and integrity to meet such adversity as was found in recent European history. But we also are realizing to an increasing degree that the individual's decision before God matters more than the phenomena of the masses as a political and social factor may make it appear. Whatever we may think about Kierkegaard's Single One before God, we should like to believe that his attributes of secret dignity and loyalty are living forces in many individuals today. The metaphysical displacements of our time are producing a wholesome effect upon many individuals, an effect that eludes the realm of statistics and may not even be represented in the political assertions of Church and organized religion.

But we must not raise such hope to the rank of an assurance. Pascal's mood in saying, "We are not yet, we hope to be," has a Kierkegaardian ring and should also be our motto. The invasion of the secular by the spiritual is God's demand upon our time. God is the God of the living, and Rilke's existential tendency to have death pervade all his creative thinking is not in harmony with Kierkegaard's concern. Kierkegaard's awareness of the luminous penetration of all spheres of life by a "lived" vision of eternity is in some ways akin to Jaspers' *Existenzerhellung*. It not only lends life clarity but also brings our guilt, littleness, and insufficiency into sharp focus like a searchlight in the night suddenly flooding a hidden scene with its brilliant illumination. Fear, anxiety, the "holy terror" of Berdyaev, the *Lebensangst* of Kafka, and the proverbial sense of suspense have, with Kierkegaard, their balance in God's love, that incomprehensible grace that dignifies life and restores victory. Man is guilty, but he is also redeemed from this guilt.

In our time, Kierkegaard's religious position has become, in a different and yet related sense, the crisis of modern man. Today man is less willing to risk the "leap" into the uncertainties of believing and is inclined to foster that assurance which reason, logic, science, or dogma are supposed to supply.

The rediscovery of Kierkegaard in France by Henri Delacroix around 1900, and about the same time in Germany where Christoph Schrempf introduced him with more enthusiasm than sound preparation, has intensified the spiritual and philosophical crisis of Europe. It has likewise inspired the crisis theology of Karl Barth and Paul Tillich, whose theology is essentially an expansion of Kierkegaard's demand that religiousness A, the belief in God's immanence present in any genuine religion, be replaced by religiousness B, the specifically Christian faith in the paradox of God's having become man in Christ. Both Barthianism and the more socially conscious neo-orthodoxy try to transmit the tragic sense of urgency inherent in Kierkegaard's message by stressing the conviction that the unique event of Christ's life on earth places ineluctable duties upon man in our time. But their messages are frequently couched in a theological biblicism unacceptable to large and serious-minded segments of Christianity. The mood of the modern Christian is divided between his vastly expanded scientific insights and the intellectually recognized need for a new inwardness. It sees in Kierkegaard's demand for the uncritical faith of Job and Abraham a leap into a blind trust for which the faint echoes of William James' "will to believe" and his social anxieties hardly supply adequate spiritual energies.

Kierkegaard's Either-Or is still (or again) our dilemma. His reproach that Christianity's real enemies are not atheists but we ourselves, the silent apostates who are preparing the end of Christianity, is now even truer than in his time. He would consider our contrasting an atheistic Russia with the "Christian" West part of our grand strategy of "Christian" self-deception, or he would perhaps call it an outright act of hypocrisy. For him there must be nothing between Christ and the Antichrist, whereas large segments of Christianity insist on remaining forever in the twilight zone of an indifferent Christian respectability. Indifference was, in the verdict of Jesus, worse than sin, and in our time Nicholas Berdyaev has coined the phrase that "average goodness is no longer enough."

No wonder that the breakdown of Europe's civilization was heralded thirty years after Kierkegaard's life with renewed force and in a different manner by the vitalism of Friedrich Nietzsche, whose worship of life and whose pagan flight into antiquity delivered into the hands of a self-satisfied middle class the convenient argument that he, too, was an eccentric and deserved no serious attention. This same obtuseness is again operating in our time when we minimize the symptomatic importance of contemporary existentialism.

Chapter 16

DID KIERKEGAARD FORGET God's mercy and forgiveness? Did he onesidedly emphasize guilt, sin, and God's remoteness from man?

We shall have to say a word about this in the concluding chapter. For the moment we may let the total impact of his numerous sermons with their emphasis on God's love reply with a clear "no." The state of Christianity was such that he had to shout, as he once said, like the chief of a fire company in the midst of a conflagration of indifference, cowardice, evil, and outright disbelief.

Kierkegaard is the pilgrim to the Absolute. The almost hysterical insistence of his message has some of the terrifying impact of Savonarola's sermons in the Florence of the fifteenth century. "You speak as though we all will go to hell and only you will be saved," once said Bishop Martensen to him. But Kierkegaard wrote that in the religious sphere "the positive is known by the negative . . ." and his solace to the despairing seeker is: "He who loves God has no need of tears nor of admiration. He forgets his suffering in love, forgets it so completely that he would not have the faintest idea of his pains if God himself did not remember them. He sees that which is hidden and knows the torment; He counts the tears and forgets nothing."

Fyodor M. Dostoevsky

> *Shatov whispered excitedly, "I believe in Russia; I believe in her orthodoxy . . . I believe that Christ's second coming will occur in Russia . . . I believe . . ."*

Chapter 1

AMONG THE TWENTY-ONE condemned men to be shot for revolutionary activities at seven o'clock on the morning of December 22, 1849, was Fyodor Dostoevsky. They were led out into the prison yard to stand on the scaffold, and the officer in charge read to each the fatal words of the verdict, "Sentenced to be shot!" The prisoners' clothes had been taken off, and for twenty minutes they waited in the ice-cold temperature for the final moment to come. Dostoevsky embraced two of his friends in a last farewell. He wrote later of this "last" moment, "I kept staring at a church with a gilt dome reflecting the sunbeams and I suddenly felt as if these beams came from the region where I myself was going to be in a few minutes."

Suddenly an officer came galloping across the square, signalling with a handkerchief to announce that Tsar Nicholas I, "in his infinite mercy," had commuted the death sentence to prison terms in Siberia. This cruel staging of the execution had been intended as "a lesson never to be forgotten." It had, indeed, a lasting effect and not only on Dostoevsky. Grigoriev, one of the condemned men, became insane; others suffered nervous breakdowns, contracted incurable diseases of the lungs, or had their ears and toes frozen. Dostoevsky did not remember having felt the cold at all.

These minutes were one of those terrifying, ultimate experiences to which his writings frequently refer. All the agonies which another Russian writer, Leonid Andreiev, describes so vividly in his short novel *The Seven Who Were Hanged,* were there, notably the contraction of life to a last, agonizing panorama before death comes to wipe out all hope, guilt, and memory. It is no wonder that Dostoevsky's epilepsy has been traced to this terrible moment as much as to his Siberian imprisonment, although he apparently had his first seizure as a boy after hearing that his father had been murdered.

On this December morning, young Dostoevsky had been on the brink of despair and death in an experience that was not only to shape his own work but was also to give to all mankind an insight into the depth of human error and suffering. For Dostoevsky could convey this with more power than practically any other writer.

Fyodor M. Dostoevsky was born in Moscow in 1821, the same year in which Gustave Flaubert, also an epileptic, was born in a similar milieu. Dostoevsky's father, an ex-army surgeon, was employed in a hospital for the poor, and the family occupied an apartment in one of the hospital buildings. This environment of poverty and misery made a lasting impression on the boy. The family had scarcely any cultural interests. His father, who was an erratic and irritable alcoholic, acquired a small farm in the Tula region, where he treated his few serfs so badly that they murdered him when Fyodor was sixteen years of age.

At seventeen, Fyodor entered the St. Petersburg college for military engineering, where he soon withdrew from the company of his socially superior comrades, spending his time in reading all of the poetry and novels available. The range of his reading was enormous, of uneven merit, and hardly suited to shape his critical judgment. He read Homer, Shakespeare, Goethe, Schiller, Corneille, Racine, Gogol, and Victor Hugo, in addition to a weird assortment of melodramatic and historical fiction.

St. Petersburg remained an unreal, "magical vision, a dream" that gave him the first vague "hints and tokens" of the strange human scene of whose description he was soon to become a master. He had no share in the city's social life and was not admitted to the circles of government officials. But he absorbed the magic of the city's icy nights and the remote human climate of its men and women with a psychic intuition that set his soul to searching after the hidden, the strange, and the darkly romantic.

After graduation Dostoevsky decided to abandon a military career in favor of writing. His first work, *Poor Folk,* was enthusiastically acclaimed by leading critics. But his initial luck as a writer vanished with the publication of his next two or three novels, profound as they were in their psychological insight. In April, 1849, Dostoevsky was arrested as a member of a socialistic group of middle-class liberals interested in Fourier's theories, and a little more than half a year later, there occurred the staging of the execution that was followed by four years of imprisonment in Omsk, Siberia.

These years brought to him more than anguish and terror. The young writer's extraordinary resilience caused him, years later, to remark rather boastfully, "I have the vitality of a cat." He displayed it even at the moment when he left for Siberia. Before his actual departure he wrote to his beloved brother Mikhail of the "abundant and healthy kind of spiritual life" seething in him as it never had before. "I shall be born again for the best. That is all my hope, all my comfort." There was no complaint about his punishment and suffering, both of which he readily accepted. In much the same way many characters in his later novels were to confess their sins and do penance for the purification of their souls.

His *Memoirs of the House of the Dead* is a harrowing description of his years in the filthy Siberian prison, where he had to live in the company of thieves, murderers, and other criminals. Yet his attitude toward his fellow prisoners was often one of real sympathy and curiosity. His comrade in chains on the way to Siberia, a Polish fellow prisoner, Jastrzembski, thus expressed himself about Dostoevsky: "It was Dostoevsky's friendly and helpful conversation that saved me from despair . . . his sensitiveness, his delicacy of feeling, his playful sallies—all this exercised a calming influence upon me. . . . Dostoevsky belonged to the cate-

gory of those beings of whom Michelet has said that 'while
the bravest of males, they have at the same time much of
the feminine nature.' " The two men parted in tears at
Tobolsk.

The contacts with the Siberian prisoners left their mark
on almost every one of Dostoevsky's later writings. As an
intellectual he was shunned by most of his fellow prisoners,
but he made the strange discovery that among these outcasts there were "deep, strong, and beautiful natures, won-
derful people," the victims of forces over which they had
no control. Nietzsche, his later admirer, refers to Dostoevsky's observations about such men by calling them "the
type of strong men made sick."

In Siberia Dostoevsky rediscovered his faith in Christ.
He reported that God granted him at times moments of
perfect serenity and that there was nothing more beautiful,
profound, and manly than the image of Christ. Such religious affirmations did not mean that he was free from
religious doubts. But his Siberian exile, his rediscovery of
Christ, his hope for the Orthodox Church, and his fervent
devotion to Mother Russia characterize this most important
phase in Dostoevsky's religious and artistic development.

Contemporary discussion of the nature of Dostoevsky's
work seems to center around the question as to whether he
was a novelist or a prophetic visionary. He was undoubtedly both, and in the light of recent European history one
might also classify him as a clairvoyant. His religious
fervor and his art are as inseparably woven together as
are his erratic nature and the sufferings that gave him his
profound insight into human nature. Even if his characters
spoke only for themselves and not necessarily for Dostoevsky, they nevertheless represent the vision and spirit of
their time, their people, and their leaders. And this seems
to have been Dostoevsky's design. Once when speaking
about *The Possessed* he said, "I want to express certain
ideas even if the artistic factors of my work are lost."

Dostoevsky's hectic career was not ended when he was
released from the *katorga* to serve for five years in a Si-

berian line-battalion. His marriage to a widow of dubious reputation was the first of several unhappy and turbulent love experiences which tortured him as much as his many other problems, and these frustrations may account for the fact that none of his novels portray a happily married and harmonious couple.

After returning to St. Petersburg, he started in 1861 the liberal magazine *Vremia (Time),* which preached populism, the need for closer collaboration between the intelligentsia and the people, and love for the Russian soil. *Vremia* also published his *Insulted and Injured* and the *Memoirs from the House of the Dead,* both significant because of their psychological insight but of minor artistic quality. Some of Dostoevsky's smaller pieces, written as a vigorous critique of Western civilization, were also published in the same magazine.

When the magazine was suspended by order of the political authorities, Dostoevsky started on his erratic odysseys in Europe, which left him forever restless and unsettled. Gambling away borrowed money, the unending problem of appeasing his publishers, an unhappy love affair, and his inability to manage his financial predicaments made him an unhappy and homesick man. After returning to Russia, he founded another magazine entitled *Epokha (Epoch),* went bankrupt, lost his best friend, the journalist Grigoriev, his wife, and his brother Mikhail by death, and was without let-up hopelessly in debt. There followed more gambling in Germany, actual starvation, and endless financial embarrassment. Even the success of *Crime and Punishment* could not save him from these miseries. When he finally married again, he gambled away, on his two-year honeymoon in Germany, Switzerland, and Italy, even the personal belongings of his wife, and seemed several times on the brink of a complete collapse. He had, indeed, "the vitality of a cat," since he was able to produce *The Idiot* and *The Possessed* under circumstances which would have ruined the health and mind of any other writer.

Once back on Russian soil, his creative energies increased, and his wife, Anna Gregorievna, managed their finances in such a way that the final ten years of his life became a period of quiet and even of comfort, with the exception of one more conflict with the political police. His *Journal of a Writer, A Raw Youth,* and, lastly, *The Brothers Karamazov* made him, for many of his fellow countrymen, the uncontested leader of Russian thought. His famous Pushkin address, delivered half a year before his death, was a personal triumph of the highest order, fulfilling the claim of his disciples that Dostoevsky would rank among the greatest in Russian history, even, indeed, as the father of Russia's faith in her all-embracing destiny for Europe and for mankind.

His personal appearance during the last years of his life was anything but patriarchal. Nervous, emaciated, and melancholy, his face appeared a mixture of that coarseness, subtlety, and sweetness which we have come to regard as typical of the Russian peasant. All the qualities that had lived in the characters of his novels seemed engraved on his features: saintliness, criminal distortion, the marks of the believer and skeptic, the volcanic zeal of the preacher, and the resignation of the martyr. Yet his death mask shows a face of ancestral distinction. Death had bestowed a clarity upon his features which suggested the rare spiritual victory of his *via dolorosa*.

Dostoevsky has, indeed, shaped the thinking of generations, as did his contemporaries Bakunin, Tolstoy, Marx, and Darwin, all of whom wrote in one sense or another the laws for our time. Each of them—and many others—wrote his own preface to the disturbing chapters of European history as we see it unfolding in the religious, moral, and political crisis of our age.

Chapter 2

WE EXPECT THE CHARACTERS of any Russian novel to reveal traits and display reactions different from American and Western European behavior. Russia's climate and geography, with its enormous contrasts of beauty and barrenness, linked with the dramatically violent history of the country including the termination of serfdom less than sixty years before the 1917 revolution, had their share in shaping the complex Russian mind. Humor, sadness, and fatalism live close together and shade off almost imperceptibly into religious resignation; personal happiness easily becomes an all-embracing love for mankind and for the whole of creation; moral defeat, rage, poverty, humiliation, and exploitations seem to produce bizarre or eccentric as well as indignant and rebellious characters.

Many of the works of Chekhov, Turgeniev, and Leo Tolstoy are exceptions to this pattern. It is surprising how quickly they establish that easy rapport with the reader that conveys the mood of familiarity with the men and women in their stories and novels. In this respect Tolstoy is a master. His art of attributing universal human traits to any of his men, women and children and of suggesting them with photographic faithfulness in little gestures or remarks, exhibits such deft powers of characterization that they are unforgettable. He achieves the miracle of obliterating time and space between the story's figures and the reader; after a few pages the men and women in *War and Peace* become our contemporaries or neighbors. Somehow we are made to feel that we have met them or people like them. That this is also true of Turgeniev's stories is more natural because he had become so frankly westernized (as Tchaikovsky was probably Russia's most "Western" composer). Most of Gogol's characters, odd, ridiculous, or tragic as they are, arouse our sympathy as readily as Dickens' men and women. Chekhov's and Gorky's tales are filled with people hardly more extraordinary than those in any other literature. But Leonid Andreiev leads us to that borderland of human psychology where it becomes almost impossible to distinguish between eruptive emotionalism, the eerie mood of insanity, and national traits or impulses that are beyond the grasp of the uninitiated foreigner. His sixth sense for the hidden horrors in man's mind and their impending explosions lends his stories that uncanny air of mystery or catastrophe that we have come to associate with the world of Russian conspirators, anarchists, and criminals.

None of Russia's story-tellers has fused the contradiction in the Russian mind so inseparably together as Dostoevsky. His characters' penchant for self-analysis makes them no more plausible than their actions; on the contrary, it tends to increase our confusion because it is, again, excessive and disordered. They love to discuss their own psychology loudly and publicly. The beginning of Chapter 28 in *The Possessed* is characteristic of the internal mood of all his novels; it says, "Incidentally, they were less speaking than shouting at each other."

Kafka's novels transmit a feeling of abandonment and remoteness between the characters themselves and between their fate and the reader, a sensation quite different from that which Dostoevsky's overheated scenes produce. He loves to crowd us into one room with all kinds of nervous people whose excitement is suffocating. Or he makes us suddenly and without warning the witness of the solitary broodings of a sinner, a jilted lover, a criminal, or a saint. His characters seem at any moment ready to expose their most private affairs and to confess sins and crimes in the self-accusing manner that has caused American observers in our time to be skeptical of the alleged confessions in iron curtain countries. *The Idiot* (Chapter 14) contains a fascinating episode in which men and women of high society practice confession as a drawing-room pastime. It conveys such an appalling mixture of sophistication, boastfulness, cynicism, and suspicion that it would scare the last ounce of naïveté out of the joyful confessors of the Oxford Group Movement.

We have, naturally, to expect in Russian literature a background of poverty, misery, or brutality, but such conditions are by no means the chief concern of the Russians. Their classical writers of the nineteenth century defied the pattern of Western literature which pretended to have found the key to man's essence in sociological information.

At the time when Dostoevsky was writing his novels, a great deal of European literature was already under the spell of Hippolyte Taine's theory that heredity, environment, and the historic conditions of a time (in one word, the circumstances) would always determine man's character and destiny, or, as Karl Marx put it even more dogmatically, that man is the product of his environment. The naturalism of Balzac, Zola, Flaubert, Maupassant, Hauptmann, Ibsen, and Hamsun supplies ample illustration for such thinking. Sordid physical conditions and the psychological squalor for which "Zola's delight in stinking" (Nietzsche) was the oustanding example, are the mark of a great deal of this naturalistic literature.

But this does not hold true for most of Russian literature, and it is especially untrue of Dostoevsky. A story's setting may be as realistic as that in any of these Western works, but such stage properties remain secondary to the real locale in Dostoevsky's tales, which is always the soul of man. No corner of the Russian psyche remains unvisited. It is the headquarters for all and everything that happens. The soul is the stage for triumph, defeat, and suffering, and all that seems to matter in life is the consideration of what life has done or will do to man's soul.

The naturalism of Western European literature was nothing but a first and distant warning signal of the breakdown of society. A morally corroded ruling class was doomed to disappear. Dostoevsky took these shocking revelations about man's nature for granted. Man was corrupt, but there was infinitely more to say: he was also capable of greatness and even saintliness. He, too, paints social splendor or abject misery, but neither could determine man's character. Some of Dostoevsky's aristocrats have "dead-end" minds, whereas many of his social outcasts belong to the moral nobility.

The astounding confusion between beauty and viciousness in man's interior world is the recurring theme of this "morbid" Russian novelist, and the oceanic welter of passion and harmony that marks the ebb and flow of his characters arises out of that mysterious something called the human soul. It is more than the battlefield of ambition and desire; it is also the point of intersection where the divine and the human meet in conflict or in harmonious reconciliation. Eternity and time live in the soul in a torturing mood of homesickness, making his favorite characters strangers on earth or filling them with that sense of assurance that is the mark of mystical oneness and brotherhood.

Dostoevsky does not employ "build-up" techniques to describe environment or social conditions. He treats his readers almost rudely by omitting all preliminaries and applying a kind of X-ray technique that confronts them first with man's innermost thoughts without presenting reasons and explanations. His characters are "naked" people, and many belong to the *Humiliated and Offended,* a title given to one of his novels. Like the figures in the Gospel—different as they are in every other respect—they appear for all practical purposes unemployed, and we learn little or nothing about their ways of making a living. There is, to be sure, an occasional remark about poverty or some awkward financial situation, but what really matters are the internal events in their psyche. The interhuman conditions of friendship, love, hate, suspicion, and tension seem to occupy them more than anything else, and they are forever engaged in this tempestuous business of loving, hating, helping, or destroying themselves and others, in finding or losing life, in rushing headlong into the hell of despair or the heaven of happiness. Gales of resentment sweep over their thoughts and their hectic conversations. They are, moreover, philosophizing sinners, rebels, or sufferers capable of relating their experiences as though they were fascinated onlookers.

Dostoevsky's characters are, indeed, a strange gallery of men and women. There is an innocent prostitute like Sonia Semenovna, a saintly adulteress such as Sonia Andreievna, and a cardinal of the Roman Catholic Church who no longer believes in God. The "lull and deadness of order," which Dostoevsky dreaded so much all his life, is completely absent in this company.

This "lull and deadness of order" has, as Virginia Woolf once aptly remarked, filled libraries of Continental novels with marionettes whose ultimate psychology we are never permitted to know. In Dostoevsky's novels we are surprised and appalled at the behavior of his men and women, whose undisguised inward chaos breaks with the pattern of accepted behavior. They make no secret of the situation, not understood two or three generations ago when these novels appeared, that the European revolution had already begun in the hearts of men and that this chaos was to become a terrible reality in history.

This prophetic signal pointed out the shocking fact that our neat distinctions between vice and virtue were inadequate. We see how greatness and viciousness shake man at one and the same time in a moral schizophrenia always known to the New Testament but not yet discovered by the learned philosophers and psychologists of the second half of the nineteenth century. It is impossible to predict the moral course of any of Dostoevsky's characters or to know the hidden impulses of their past in a way which psychoanalysis has now revealed. Versilov, in *The Possessed,* once compared man's interior physiognomy and its lack of a permanent identity with the actual portrait of man. He says, "Photography seldom shows real resemblance; that is, of course, quite natural because the original, we ourselves, is seldom the same. The human face rarely expresses its most important traits or its characteristic qualities." So it is with the soul. As in the Gospel, the sinner and not the seemingly perfect man surprises us by emerging as the more attractive character, whereas the virtuous man may unexpectedly reveal himself as a base and despairing weakling.

All of Dostoevsky's stories belong to the literature of extreme situations. An ominous restlessness broods over the men and women in his novels. Frequently their reaction to seemingly small incidents is excessive, and events take a most unexpected turn. The hero in *The Dream of a Ridiculous Man* contemplates suicide once more after having repeatedly toyed with the idea because he has just treated a child rudely. Stavrogin, a monstrous and infernal character, rapes a child and wants to inflict punishment upon himself worse than death by marrying the half-witted and crippled Lebyadkina. Sonia, the prostitute, at long last saves the murderer Raskolnikov by reading to him the story of Lazarus' resurrection. Alyosha seeks spiritual strength from the saintly Elder Zossima before going to Grushenka, who wants to seduce him but who instead finds through him her faith in God. Christ's Second Coming, as envisioned in the classical scene with the Grand Inquisitor (*The Brothers Karamazov*), looks at first like a defeat and mute surrender to the forces of this world, whereas Satan's later appearance in the same novel makes him an interesting, almost pleasant philosopher. The "Underground Man" abuses a young prostitute and then spends the rest of the night in preaching to her and moving her to tears of repentance. A mysteriously moody young man in *The Possessed* takes delight in scandalizing society by biting into the ear of the town's leading official and pulling him by the nose. Though suspicious and deeply hurt, Pavlovitch, in *The Eternal Husband,* cannot resist the strange personal magnetism of his wife's seducer, whom he hates. Captain Lebyadkin, another sinister character in *The Possessed,* anticipates Nietzsche's advice not to forget the whip when dealing with women, by actually applying a whip to the nervous disorders of his sister in order to "straighten her out."

At the most dramatic moments these men and women

find time for some hectic philosophical or religious discourse, and quantities of psychological dynamite seem to lie ready to explode at any time. Even when a catharsis has occurred, one never knows what will happen next. Versilov becomes ascetic after a wild indulgence in sex and systematically trains his will power. But he is still far from the humility of a saint, for he enjoys the sense of power over himself which his newly achieved moral strength gives him. It is hard for man to bear even his real strength without abusing it. It is also not for man to define the outreach of his virtuous actions upon the lives of others: the young Zossima's refusal to fight a duel causes a most respected citizen to confess a murder he committed many years ago.

This rise and fall from one moment to the next, this whirlwind of contradictions, in one and the same person, and this burning zest for life are apt to produce dizziness in a reader who expects a well-arranged course of action. The reading of Dostoevsky's novels is actually a kind of labor. He leaves us unsettled and confused, yet strangely moved. The men and women of these novels seem figures in a dream pageant, where everything is out of proportion or where some apocalyptic message receives a symbolical twist. Some of Dostoevsky's critics have conveniently lumped together this gallery of impetuous and gloomy people in terms such as "Asiatic" or "psychopathic," and it is true that their hallucinatory appearance lends them an air of unreality reminiscent of the weird pictures of the Czech, Alfred Kubin. But they appeal, nevertheless, to our generation in a peculiar manner because we, too, are conscious of the appalling discrepancies in the men and women of our age, discrepancies which former generations pretended not to know.

It is, therefore, far from accidental that we are today taking such an interest in Dostoevsky, since eighty years ago he foresaw the breakdown of most of Europe's middle-class standards of morality and conduct. Psychoanalysis owes him a lasting debt. It is a curious fact that Freud, the founder of modern psychoanalysis, could not bear to read

Dostoevsky's novels in his later years because the divided minds of their characters were so much like those of his own patients with whom he had been laboring during the day. In fact, for them and for Dostoevsky's characters, the subconscious mind had become the center for all impulses and decisions.

Our modern interest in painters like Kokoschka, El Greco, and Gruenewald is related to this exaggerated style of portraying human conditions. Their work, too, appears "unnatural" and is beautiful only in a higher sense because it opens up new dimensions for conveying the tortures of man's soul.

Dostoevsky's novels break the standardized laws of art which stressed a well-ordered manner of smooth storytelling. He reaches out to the mysteries of fate and God's will. As Kierkegaard had clearly stated before him, the fetish of art and the aesthetic way of life rely on impressions from the outside and contain satanic elements; art as a cult is invariably the forerunner of moral and cultural decline. The somewhat artificial story of Dr. Jekyll and Mr. Hyde demands of the reader a similar approach. Beauty and tragedy in human life can be found only in the search for God's will in His creation, where the dark, the ugly, and the sinful have been assigned a divine albeit mysterious meaning. A Russian proverb says, "Love me black as I am. When I am white everyone will love me." That is the spirit of the Gospel.

In this welter of passions, deceit, and sin, Dostoevsky's saints, Prince Myshkin, Alyosha, and Father Zossima evoke our special interest. At first their innocence seems to deprive them of the dramatic attributes which Dostoevsky's great sinners possess to an extraordinary degree. Our eyes, trained to look for shadows, search in vain for clearly defined contours. These characters are transparent; nothing is hidden; nothing needs to remain secret. And by the same token little remains hidden to them. Their eyes meet with no obstruction when searching for a man's innermost center; they have a sixth sense for truth and seem to search only for their neighbor's buried ability to rise and achieve resurrection. Myshkin and Alyosha are not the unbearably virtuous type against whom our instinct for honesty rebels, and Father Zossima speaks of his life as a young officer with the candor and humor of which only Russians are capable. Myshkin and Alyosha puzzle their environment because of their disturbing strangeness. Their inward center is not in themselves or in their society but is part of the Divine. There is something supernatural about them, and as soon as their friends feel this, they love them.

Our ordinary psychological tools fail us when we attempt to analyze these characters. It is so easy to define evil and portray the sinner with concrete accuracy because evil and sin are finite and human. But virtue, perfection, and saintliness elude us because they reach out into the infinite realm of eternity. We can only touch them slightly or sense the direction of their moving energies. The presentation of evil, in which Kierkegaard also succeeded so admirably, evokes by contrast the image of perfection. But virtue and perfection transcend the borders of psychology, and our inability to understand them when they appear in great strength is as irremediable as our incompetence fully to understand Jesus.

Like Dostoevsky himself, the Idiot experiences closeness to death each time he is seized with an attack, not knowing whether it will mark the end of his life. Alyosha's deepest insight into life comes to him from the lips of the dying Father Zossima. As Raskolnikov listens to the resurrection story of Lazarus, the "sinister catechism" of evil, his belief that everything is permitted to man, fades away in the face of death's majesty and nearness to God. The circle closes, and the extremes are fused into one truth. One has to be more than an artist or psychologist to portray such characters convincingly.

Dostoevsky did not want to be called a psychologist, declaring emphatically, "I am not a psychologist. I am a realist." But he was in truth the father of modern psychology. Nietzsche praised him rightly as the only psychologist from whom he had anything to learn; yet much of his reaction to Dostoevsky resembles that of Freud, for he says that "Dostoevsky goes against my deeper instincts." Nietzsche did not want humility recognized as a virtue.

The "magic of extremes" which had shaken Dostoevsky's personal life made him follow man into the darkest corridors of his mind, where nothing remains hidden and where the only way out is the flight into God's open arms. "Always and in everything I go to the extreme limit," says Dostoevsky of himself. Such passion for excesses leads him to the uncharted frontiers of all existence, where he would stand before the ultimate mysteries of life revealed only by faith. "The ant knows the formula of its abode and work . . . but man does not," he once wrote. God alone can lead him.

Chapter 3

DOSTOEVSKY'S ERRATIC TRAVELS in Germany, France, and Switzerland, where he went to escape from his debtors and to try his luck at roulette, left him each time as wretched and homesick as Prince Myshkin in *The Idiot,* full of yearning for Mother Russia. Europe, this "beautiful cemetery," filled him with fear. Certain aspects of the London World's Fair (1851) created in him forebodings of an oncoming world disaster of biblical dimensions, akin to the terrifying sense of doom which the Apostles felt when they heard Jesus' prophecies about the fate of Jerusalem's splendor. The civilization of cities—those cities which Rilke later called "disordered and dissolved"—and in particular modern industrialism, frightened Dostoevsky; he regarded both as the signs of another Fall of Man. London was the new Babylon, and the accumulation of wealth and power there was to him a symbol of man's rebellious pride against God.

Dostoevsky gave his pessimism an apocalyptic note when he said that the end of the world was approaching, and the "end of this century will be seen in disorders as never before." Forty years before the outbreak of the First World War he was convinced that Europe stood on the brink of a moral and political catastrophe, a collapse "that will be without exception, general, and terrible. This ant heap without a Church and Christianity . . . is already practically undermined. The fourth estate (the lower classes) is rising; it will smash the door. . . . Catholicism having ceased to be Christian is turning into pagan idolatry; Protestantism is fast approaching atheism." He couched his accusations in vehement terms: "There is no more universal idea! Everything is flabby, vapid, all people are vapid! We all, we all, are empty!"

Such ultimate visions as those expressed by Shigailev, one of the characters in *The Possessed,* are all the more

uncanny because we have since witnessed the actual decomposition of society in Central Europe; we are unfor-
tunately in a position to realize the prophetic truth in
Dostoevsky's conclusions. Over eighty years ago he predicted that the unbridled freedom of the individual would
be replaced by despotism in the future synthetic society.
One tenth of mankind would rule over the other nine-
tenths, who would lose all individual personality and become a kind of working herd, quite in accord with the
visions of the Grand Inquisitor and Nietzsche. This élite
body of supermen is precisely the group which, according
to the Grand Inquisitor, is alone capable of "bearing freedom"; these are the supermen of whom the devil says to
Ivan Karamazov, "A single soul like that weighs as much
as a whole astronomical system—we have our own arith-
metical scale!" Raskolnikov, the murderer, becomes an
early forerunner of this evil gospel when he divides
mankind into ordinary and extraordinary people and
"sentences" to death the pawnbroker, his first victim.

But it was not only Europe that appeared doomed. Dostoevsky had also his specific fears for Russia's future.
Everywhere in Europe he had met uprooted fellow countrymen who were rushing about as aimlessly as he was himself, haunted by restlessness or living as political fugitives
and waiting for tomorrow's revolution; they were the "rats
getting off the sinking ship." Dostoevsky felt for them only
pity and indignation. They did not know how to behave in
public. They spoke in a loud manner when they ought to
have been silent; they were incapable of politeness or simple, natural behavior when such was expected of them.
Their belief that the West could ever become their spiritual home was fallacious; they had fled from Russia's future
Golden Age when Asia might yet become Russia's main
outlet. They were déracinés.

But such asides about Russia were brief, and Dostoevsky's passionate anger was mainly directed against Europe.
Her great powers would be destroyed. The moral sub-

stance of that continent was worn out and undermined by the repressed democratic urges of the poor and exploited, whereas Russia still possessed an inexhaustible reservoir of strength in her plain and unbroken people, a rather optimistic view taken with the full knowledge of the suppression and poverty rampant in Russia! Turgeniev had dismissed his own country as barbarian, amounting to literally nothing in the world's cultural and industrial progress, but Dostoevsky, in spite of dark forebodings, believed firmly in Russia's spiritual mission for the world. The very future of Europe would belong to Russia.

There were, to be sure, contradictions in this sweeping condemnation of Western nations. Dostoevsky was generous and forgiving toward sinners and criminals but harsh in his thinking as a nationalist. Such limitations recall the aging Tolstoy, whose artistic genius had blinded him to the realities of the world he set out to reform. The weird mixture of prophecy, fear, condescension, and outright hate for Western civilization, his dark pain and anger, came from the same psychological wounds from which always he had long suffered; to his dying day he deeply resented the application of the epithet "Asiatic" to his own country and its civilization. When shortly before his death he appealed to the Russian people to turn to Asia ("Asia will be our civilization!"), this call carries the fury of an enormous resentment. Asia, so he thought, would supply the means and resources for ruling the world, an idea disquieting our generation as much as his claims for Russia's messianic role.

Dostoevsky had seen the signs of decay everywhere in Germany, France, and Switzerland, but he lacked the historic perspective to do justice to the great ideas of individual freedom rising in those nations and to the role of reason in religion and politics. He thought in terms of the anonymous mass man, the man of tomorrow, and endowed him lavishly with the mystical qualities of a collective soul that was to be the medium of a superpersonal and divine will. The individual would be carried along in the stream of time and events, like grains of sand rolling on to the banks and beaches of the future. Bakunin's attack upon Europe was couched in terms of political anarchism, but when Dostoevsky speaks of Europe's middle classes, he calls them stupid, ignorant, bored, mediocre, and cheating. Europe's moribund Catholicism was worse than atheism. He extended his verdict on Europe's "tottering" society to liberalism in religion and politics, both of which he considered mere symptoms of decay. Liberalism, he believed, could produce only skepticism, atheism, and political nihilism. It is significant that Verkhovensky, the typical liberal in *The Possessed,* had a nihilistic son, and Ivan Karamazov, the rationalist and atheist, was the seducer of his half-witted brother, who murdered his father.

In retrospect we can now readily see the truth in some of his diagnoses; we also know that the unconscious and unawakened mind of the Russian masses was no alternative to the excesses of Continental liberalism. The real solution to Europe's ills was and still is, not a return to paternalism and Orthodox tradition, but the development of a responsible and self-disciplined sense of freedom under the guidance of Christian faith. Dostoevsky's thinking of man in "we" terms was typically Russian and Slavic. As Bakunin had said, "I do not want to be I, I want to be We." The conscious claim for individual rights remained alien to Dostoevsky also.

In fairness to him it must be admitted, however, that much of his criticism was justified. The European intelligentsia had, in effect, proudly detached themselves from the masses, had become "déracinés," and had lost touch with their own people. A generation after Dostoevsky, and too late to retrieve what had been lost, Maurice Maeterlinck made the remarkable statement that the thinker continues to think justly only as he does not lose contact with those who do not think at all. And in our own time, Julien Benda's sensational book about the treason of the intellectuals (*La Trahison des Clercs*) raises the same reproach against the ivory tower existence of the highly educated.

Needless to say, events of our time have confirmed the truth of much in Dostoevsky's diagnoses. History has spoken a harsh verdict on Europe's civilization. In retrospect it is, however, of more than historical interest to remember that most of the truly enlightened or democratic leaders in France, Germany, England, and Denmark came from the intelligentsia and the middle classes. Even revolutionists like Karl Marx, Lassalle, Engels, and the older Liebknecht spoke out against their own middle class with more political authority than Dostoevsky himself. Russia's own bourgeoisie produced historians and social reformers who chastised their fatherland for its brutality and backwardness with more detachment than Dostoevsky's nationalistic fervor ever allowed him to do. Alexander Herzen, the exiled rebel, wrote in 1851, that the European chaos would be accelerated by Russia, his fatherland, which he spoke of as "a hostile, threatening state . . . an impatient heir ready to accelerate its slow death." Dostoevsky seemed to speak from a robust nationalism without noting the voices of revolutionaries and historians who foresaw Russia's great mission for Europe's future with no less fervor than he. In their minds Russia's victory over Napoleon (1812) had established her undisputable claim to determine Europe's future destiny. Chaadayev declared in 1830 that Russia had not yet given anything to humanity; all her energies were as yet held in reserve, but in the future she would lead mankind. Such dreams revived the peculiar mystique expressed in Tyutchev's poem (1860) which proclaimed that Russia cannot be understood or measured with a common yardstick; one must *believe* in Russia.

Dostoevsky shared this belief with Pushkin, and both were convinced that Russia's unique genius was her ability to understand Western civilization by intuition. *Ex oriente lux!* In 1836, one year before his death, Pushkin had written that Russia was Europe's court of arbitration. The Russians were to be the great and unprejudiced judges with their "healthy sense for realities about everything that is not happening with us" (*sic*). Russian Christendom, free from Western skepticism and flabby liberalism, held an enormous reservoir of spiritual power in her people. Dostoevsky's famous speech in honor of Pushkin elaborated on the poet's thought by stating that the whole Russian nation not only had the ability to understand the spirit of other nations but also the urge to be their future reconciler. To be a true and genuine Russian meant to be a brother to all men; the historic speech also envisioned the future fraternal union of all peoples according to the law of Christ.

These are major claims, which are all the more uncanny in the light of recent events in Europe and Asia. Dostoevsky was opposed to socialism and dictatorship; yet he has substantially contributed to the nationalistic fanaticism that saved Russia from Hitler but has since been employed by her rulers for enlarging Russian imperialism, just as the nationalism of the 1870's and 1880's was accustomed to drape itself in the garb of divine mission. It is more than a coincidence that one of the forefathers of German nationalism, the poet Ernst Moritz Arndt, had preached an equally fervent and religious patriotism decades before Germany had even been united. Arndt advocated a universalism quite similar to that of the Russians. As early as 1843 he also called the German a citizen of the world, a universal man, "to whom God has given the whole earth as a home." Prussian nationalism was at that time as utopian as Pushkin's and Dostoevsky's later ideas must have appeared to many observers; yet our own time has seen how realistic the dreams of poets and writers can become.

The enormous reservoir or spiritual power in Russia's plain people was Dostoevsky's romantic obsession, as it was also the fervent hope of other Russian writers, especially of Leo Tolstoy, who never tired of endowing the untutored peasant with saintlike attributes. One hears a late echo of Rousseau's praise of the *beau sauvage* in this elevation of the humble *mushjik* to the position of anonymous yet ever-present messiah. The historian Khomyakov also based his messianic claims for Russia's destiny upon the "fact" that the Russians are the most humble people; and Dostoevsky's later panslavism is nothing but the logical extension of this messianic hope to the wider racial community of Eastern Europe. We know now how dangerous such pride in humility can become.

Strangely enough and in contrast to many of Tolstoy's characters, Dostoevsky's men and women are city people, even when they live, like the Karamazovs, in the country. Dostoevsky himself was a man of the city, though his work abounds in praise of the soil and its sacramental nature. The compensation for the disgust aroused by the human products of metropolitan decay is his great love for the plain people, which permeated his books at a time when Karl Marx spoke disdainfully of the "idiocy of rural life." Dostoevsky wrote, "One has to grow on the soil where the corn and trees are growing," and from which "the whole order, freedom, life, honor, the family, the children, the church—in one word, everything of value comes." He believed that in this God-given order alone could grow the true communion of man.

The sense of universal fellowship with all creatures, so characteristic of Dostoevsky's novels, clearly has its root in this love for the soil, this precious Russian soil, the new Galilee pregnant with the most immediate religious expectancy. "The Russian people are a God-bearing people," he wrote, and it was only logical that they would expect Christ's second coming to happen in Russia. In the legend of the Grand Inquisitor the Spaniards who kiss the soil that Jesus' feet had touched are in reality Russians. Maria Lebyadkina in *The Possessed* knows that the Russian soil is God's own mother, the "prodigiously bearing one," and every evening she kisses the earth when saying her prayers. The earth from which all sinners come and to which they return is a sacramental symbol; Raskolnikov kisses "that filthy earth" in supernatural joy after confessing his crimes. Even the ethereal Myshkin, the saintly city hero of *The Idiot,* says, "He who has no soil of his own has also no God." The fatherly Elder Zossima believes that atheists will only be converted by the power of the plain people and suggests to the saintly Alyosha, "Make it a habit to fall down and kiss the earth! Kiss the earth and always love it . . . love everything and everybody . . . do not feel ashamed of your ecstasy. . . ." And after his advisor's death Alyosha follows this counsel in unrestrained enthusiasm. Without wanting to reflect on his action, he kissed the earth, sobbing silently, drenching it with his tears. He was beyond himself and vowed to love the soil, love it to all eternity. Even the death of the revered Elder is nothing but an embrace of the soil. The old man slipped off the chair, spreading his arms "as though he were kissing the soil in joyful ecstasy."

Dostoevsky is, of course, not the only one to praise the Russian soil. There are, for example, scenes in Tolstoy's stories reminiscent of the same attitude (*Father Sergius!*), and while his reverence carries a note of pantheism, it ranks high above the later blood-and-soil paganism of the Nazis. In fact, it has some of the poetic traits we find associated with saints like St. Francis of Assisi. Makar in *A Raw Youth* praises the leaves of grass, God's "little grass," God's children—everything belongs to God. There are mysterious bonds with God's other worlds, from which the seeds have been taken for our own garden of life, and only reverence and a thankful heart will understand the puzzle of our existence within God's mysterious design. Everything is part of it, and when Alyosha falls asleep at the coffin of his departed spiritual father, Zossima, "the vast dome of heaven, covered with the silent, glittering stars" and the milky ways reaching from one end of the universe to the other were becoming the absolute evidence that he belonged to both worlds, the visible of man and the invisible one of God. The egotism of the "I" shrinks to nothingness in view of this cosmic grandeur, and the "We" replaces it with the knowledge that the Russian people as a body also have a God-given destiny.

In Dostoevsky's thinking the soil not only produces the beauty of Russia and the fruits of her labor, but it is the one element that ties all Russians together in the sight of God. The rich and the poor, the learned and the virtuous are all part of this sacramental community. The soil has kept them together in spite of unbearable political and social tensions. Miracles abound in this land, and God is at work in His own way. No wonder that bold hopes attach themselves to a belief in God's own intervention such as arose from the childlike faith of the early Christians. The Kingdom of God will be established after the Second Coming of Christ, a new order for which especially the landless peasants were waiting, an order "which will be entirely different." "Our Father," the opening words of the Lord's Prayer, are a prophetic petition, as Nicholas Berdyaev once explained. Some day God will actually be the Father of a united mankind, and Moscow will be the Third Rome, the spiritual center of all believers everywhere. Such ultimate hopes were not only a living creed among the peasants but also among numerous theologians and philosophers before and after Dostoevsky's time, men like Chaadayev, Kireyevsky, Khomyakov, Ivan and Konstantin Aksakov, and others.

But the faithful do not need to wait indefinitely. The priesthood of all believers is already mysteriously present in this community of hope, and the Elder Zossima teaches in sincere happiness that the Kingdom is upon all those who will open their eyes to this supreme truth. It is here! Life as a paradise is no longer a vague hope but an actuality, and the Elder encourages the people to be joyful "like children and the birds of heaven." The joyful can never be godless, as Dostoevsky says in *A Raw Youth*. This naïve and innocent pleasure in life is nothing less than the testimony of the pure in heart, the only ones privileged to see God.

Chapter 4

DOSTOEVSKY HAD SAID to himself that without the Russian earth "all my strength, all my talent will dry up," and it was his conviction that man's spiritual catastrophe would be inescapable when he loses his ties with the soil, the people, and humanity. Alienation from God would be the logical consequence of such a detachment. This absence of faith results in a revolt against God's moral law and in man's arrogant claim to rule his own destiny.

Dostoevsky has no academic arguments to offer for faith, but leads us, like Dante, through the hellish tortures of those who have abandoned it. In some instances, intellectual atheism received short shrift in Dostoevsky's novels and in his other writings. He makes, for example, Nicholas Vsevolodovitch in *The Possessed* say, "An atheist can't be a Russian; an atheist ceases at once to be a Russian." Shatov, in the same novel, remarks, "Russian atheism has never proceeded beyond the joking stage." Kirillov's statement echoes some Darwinian thinking when he expresses the fear that mankind might now descend from God to the gorilla since it has risen from the gorilla to God. And Peter Verkhovensky (*The Possessed*) makes the prophetic statement about Russia's future, that "a Russian revolution will unfailingly start with atheism." Religion was to Dostoevsky so much a part of Russia's climate and geography that the Russians would make "a religion of atheism if they ever embraced it."

But his thinking is more universal than this close tie between religion and patriotism might indicate. Shortly before his death, a woman correspondent complained to him that the road to clarity and moral freedom was a painful struggle and a never-ending conflict. His rather impatient reply was, "What are you writing me of your inner conflicts? To have these is obviously the trait of all humans—that is of all those who are above the ordinary. . . . It causes great pains but also extreme joy."

His novels dramatize this duality in man and illustrate his conviction that a life lived only according to human self-direction will invariably lead to a subhuman existence. Man must not be reconciled to himself. This note is always the same whether we follow the megalomaniac student Raskolnikov into the criminal hinterlands of his mind, or see Ivan Karamazov and his father sink in debaucheries, or watch Dimitry indulge in unbridled eroticism, or hear the demon-ridden Kirillov cry out, "God has pursued me all my life." It is a despair akin to Kierkegaard's fear and trembling and Faust's "two souls residing in my breast." These vacillations between light and darkness make young Arkady in *A Raw Youth* ask himself how it is that the basest motives in man can exist side by side with the utmost sincerity and purity.

The powers of reason, which had been exalted for almost a century before Dostoevsky dramatized this struggle between the light and darkness, had proved incapable of solving this breach in man's personality. Logic, intelligence, and reason could not master the dark forces in man that had a volition of their own and a hidden purpose. The *mysterium iniquitatis* is more than ordinary moral guilt; it is a metaphysical problem. Man is bound to be guilty; our reasoning judgment can only intensify our pain, not relieve it. For "the good that I would I do not; but the evil which I would not, that I do" (Romans VII:19).

It is, indeed, a mystery, and atheism has exploited it as thoroughly as possible. But reasoning and understanding, both divinely created, cannot comprehend their creator, and the mystery is not solved by calling it nonsense. Nicholas Berdyaev sums up the essence of Dostoevsky's faith by stating that the existence of evil proves God's existence. A wholly good and righteous world would have no need for God, "for the world itself would be god." And he concludes that God is because evil exists, "and that means that God is because freedom is."

Guilt and sin, then, are an existential condition of man, and the problem of human guilt is central in Dostoevsky's thinking. His typically Russian emphasis on man as a collective being leads logically to his belief in our all-guilt; we are, again, in some mysterious manner, guilty of everybody's sins, and the numerous public confessions in the stories of Dostoevsky and other Russian writers are, therefore, quite understandable, grotesque or repulsive as they must appear to us. Our own deeds, good or bad, are nothing but pebbles in the river of life that will be carried on and on until they somehow touch our remotest fellow man. The individual is nothing and—everything, and Makar includes in his prayers all those for whom nobody ever prays.

But there is also the *mysterium caritatis*. Not only does our guilt affect our fellow man; our forgiveness and love are equally pervasive. Father Zossima's story of the duel and of the influence he unwittingly exercised upon the mysterious stranger who confessed a murder, is the most telling illustration for this belief. It finds, incidentally, an interesting parallel in Tolstoy's *Father Sergius,* written almost twenty years later.

Dostoevsky's plots have no solution in our sense of the word. Their solutions are spiritual, and the dominant theme is resurrection. This he has in common with the more Western Tolstoy, who is so different from him in many regards. Tolstoy's resurrection theme repeats itself in the spiritual clarity gained by his favorite characters, such as Nekhlyudov, Andrey, Pierre, Ivan Ilyitch, and others. Resurrection occupies a more central position in Russian thinking than elsewhere, as the Russian word for it (*voskresenye*) covers not only resurrection but also Sunday and Easter. It is no accident that the reading of the Lazarus story precedes Raskolnikov's confession and that the dying Makar in *A Raw Youth* as well as Zossima in *The Brothers Karamazov* radiate a light that invades the souls of their fellow men. The past is buried ("only where there are graves can resurrection be," says Nietzsche), and the future is all that counts.

The sinner is part of God's mysterious design; and there are moments when a truly divine light appears over the most abject scenes of misery, as, for example, when Marmaladov, the alcoholic father of Sonia, the prostitute, breaks out in visionary ecstasy about Judgment Day. He knows that God will call to Himself the drunkards, the weak, the sinners, the "swine," and tell the wise and prudent ones that He is calling the sinners to Him "because not one of them considered himself worthy of it." Then, so he believes, will all men understand "everything," and God's Kingdom will indeed reign. Unlike Tolstoy, who demanded the abolition of all courts of justice, Dostoevsky considers man's judgeship over man a necessity, but all judgments have to be passed in humility and love. The jury sentencing Dimitry consists of people socially and intellectually his inferiors, the "little peasants," and none of those clever Western arguments of milieu and heredity are valid before God. The real community is aware of our all-guilt, a state of mind present only in the Church. We must never cease loving the sinner because God always continues to love him. True love and justice will prevail only when God's forgiveness speaks through man's humility and no thoughts of moral superiority must ever enter our hearts.

Such thinking was alien to Nietzsche. In denying the existence of true humility, Nietzsche once remarked, "The believer feels superior to the unbeliever. I shall believe in Christian humility when I see how a believer humbles himself before the unbeliever." Dostoevsky supplied striking answers to this challenge, of which he probably never had heard; the Elder Zossima kisses the old Karamazov after his most repulsive behavior in the monastery; the returning Christ kisses the Grand Inquisitor, who has been arrogant enough to reprove and threaten Him; Alyosha kisses his cynical brother after the reading of the Grand Inquisitor's story. Western critics have called these scenes unacceptable because they were "going too far." But the most Western philosopher, Nietzsche himself, had demanded just this proof for the existence of true humility.

Dostoevsky goes further than this. The sinner is repeatedly made the medium of forgiveness and salvation for others sinners. In their childlike simplicity and honesty the common people understand sin and guilt and are ready to forgive; they are a supremely religious body, and God may choose to use any of them for His purposes. Christ is on the road in Russia and may meet anyone in the disguise of a pilgrim or a wretched hobo, one of the miracle-working *stranniks,* of which perhaps the corrupt Rasputin was the last sinister example.

Logic and human reasoning are inadequate to comprehend truth, and in this emphasis Dostoevsky speaks entirely the language of Kierkegaard, of whom he had never heard. Christianity is a way of life, an existential condition. The Elder Zossima advises a doubting woman that there is in religious matters "nothing to prove." She will, so he assures her, become convinced of God's reality and the immortal state of her soul to the degree that she progresses in practicing love. Atheists fail to see this, yet we should not despise them, so the saintly Elder warns us, because there are many good men among them, especially in modern times.

Again like Kierkegaard, who affirmed that suffering is the climate in which man's soul begins to breathe. Dostoevsky stresses the function of suffering as part of God's revelation of truth to man. The prosperous and emotionally harmonious have never passed through this gate of hell; they can, therefore, not understand their fellow men who suffer. This emphasis on suffering rises from the pages of nineteenth-century literature as part of our image of the Russian people, and becomes in turn a vast ocean of misery, a grace from heaven, a virtue, an asset of the Russian "universal man." He will always suffer and crucify himself as long as there is one single human being who suffers, and Dostoevsky even says that Russian happiness is bound to contain some suffering, without which it would not be complete. Confession is only part of it and rises from the irrepressible urge to make others share in the experience of torturing guilt. The list of those confessing sins and crimes is long and varied: Raskolnikov, Nelly, Nastasia, Foma Fomitch, the mysterious stranger visiting the young Zossima, Arkady, Stavrogin, in addition to others who confess without being guilty, like the prisoner Nikolay shouting out his confession of the murder that had been committed by Raskolnikov. And these make by no means a complete roster of Dostoevsky's confessors.

Even the grandiose and worldy wise fascism of the cardinal is in more than one sense a confession. Christ's return to this world in Seville, Spain, in the days of the Inquisition is no Second Coming in the glorious setting of the ruler who at long last comes into his own. The many paradoxes of this scene start with Jesus' arrest by the Grand Inquisitor. There could hardly be a more apt confirmation for the claim of Kierkegaard and Nietzsche that our Christian authorities are no longer Christian than to see the cardinal (the Church) arrest Jesus. While the simple people kneel down and worship the returning Christ, the cardinal knows better; tomorrow they will come to watch the doomed prisoner burn at the stake. Man wants neither God nor Christ: he wants the authority of the Church.

It is, of course, symbolical that it is an atheist who tells this story in which the cardinal defends the practices of the Church. The atheist's logical sequence is materialism and the conviction that man is too weak to live a life in God. He wants the physical security of bread; he seeks the spiritual security of dogma, of proof, or the truth of miracles. To believe in God and to undertake to follow Him irrespective of the consequences—that is too much of a risk to take, as the Grand Inquisitor suggests. The Church gives a man a lighter burden to carry; it preaches, explains, and selects the truth, forgives sins, and bestows the happiness of children upon man. The price demanded for this is high; man must surrender his freedom of thought, but he willingly does so. He no longer serves God as God may demand of him but as the Church tells him. God's mysteries and miracles will henceforth be monopolized and administered by the Church.

The political implications of the Legend are now, of course, of the greatest interest to us who have witnessed mass tragedies of the broadest dimensions. The Inquisitor's verdict about the fickle masses, the men and women who will always exchange their freedom for bread; his own confession of unhappiness; and, finally, Alyosha's verdict that the cardinal no longer represents faith but unbelief, surround the exciting Legend with a sense of prophetic accusation. For the cardinal, God had died, as Nietzsche was to proclaim only a very few years later in the first part of *Thus Spake Zarathustra*. The cardinal could no longer believe in man because he had given up believing in God. Even so did the dictators of recent history reduce or eliminate their scruples about the treatment of their fellow beings by first removing religious considerations from their hearts. Like the cardinal, they employed the fascination of economic miracles, the mysteries of thought control, and an unchecked authority. Dostoevsky's Legend of the Grand Inquisitor expresses with equal clarity his opposition to the Roman Catholic Church, political dictatorship, and communism.

The scene between Christ and the Grand Inquisitor is, incidentally, a powerful example of the indirect communication which Dostoevsky has less consciously employed than Kierkegaard and Nietzsche. The cardinal as the advocate of evil is quite verbose; he appears logical and persuasive; his arguments are saturated with worldly-wise experience. But Christ remains mute. Truth exists by its own majesty. Its mysterious language is silence.

Dostoevsky's criticism of the Church and his penchant for psychological treatment of religious and moral conflicts should, however, not make us forget that he was all his life a believer in the mission of the Church. It may be safe to say that he loved the Church more for what it might have been, or yet become, than for what it represented in its actuality. His love for the Church was an unhappy one, and it may be symbolical that some of his sinners or abnormal characters are able to minister to their fellow men with more profound effect than ordained priests. Obviously the wisdom of the Church is confounded, and those living on the margin of respectable society are also God's spokesmen. Yet, critical as Dostoevsky was of the Church, we may conclude from the scene in which Jesus kisses the Grand Inquisitor that he considered this kiss a sign of absolution from guilt, or at least a magnificent promise.

Was Dostoevsky a believer?

It is impossible to answer this question. He loved his atheists and seemed to cherish their arguments; in fact, we know how proud he was of cynical Ivan's powerful figure. Certainly Dostoevsky was no firm believer of the naïve and unshaken kind. He had gone through "a furnace of doubt." But his oscillations between believing and doubting suggest a wrestling with faith alien to an avowed atheist.

His contradictions were too passionate and tense to allow an easy answer. We are left to conclude from his art of dramatizing darkness how much he longed for the light. A doubter of his proportions is always a believer also at certain moments of his life. But it is safe to assume that he always loved Christ. He even went so far as to state that he would choose Christ even if it could be proved that Christ was not the truth.

The Orthodox faith in the immortality of the soul is a favorite topic in the conversations of several of his characters, who stress that a moral life on earth becomes senseless without the balancing justice after death; in fact, one might as well commit suicide to end all of life's miseries if there were no hereafter. But while this compensating justice in eternity will strengthen us here and now, the

Kingdom is already here for those who have eyes to see and ears to hear. The Elder Zossima sees the breach between God and man and between the state and the Church healed in the communion of all believers "at the end of the centuries," when it will bring about a magnificent paradise. Already, now, "life is a paradise, and all of us are in the paradise if we only would realize this. If we only would see this, then the paradise would rise tomorrow all over the world . . . not only in our ideas but in reality."

Russian Orthodoxy has never recognized a dualism between Church and world or time and eternity; nor does it admit a rupture between the two worlds of spirit and matter. The Church itself is that point in the creation where the two meet and are reconciled "in a new spirituality within the world" that has crossed the invisible boundaries between time and eternity and expands our vision beyond measure.

Friedrich Nietzsche

> *I love the great despisers. Man is something that has to be surpassed.*

Chapter 1

IT WAS CONSIDERED a good omen that the church bells were ringing on October 15, 1844, when Friedrich Nietzsche was born in Roecken, the son of a Lutheran minister and grandson of two clergymen. Prussia was celebrating the King's birthday, and when father Nietzsche baptized his son, he christened him with the King's own name, Friedrich Wilhelm. On that occasion the happy father gave a brief speech, praising himself for the privilege of being able to baptize his own child and recalling that for a number of years the month of October had always been a season of good luck for him. His heart was full of gratitude, but the speech, as quoted by Nietzsche's sister Elisabeth, forgot entirely to mention Nietzsche's mother, who was later to witness the agony of Friedrich's mental breakdown and to survive the unhappy philosopher.

His father died when Friedrich Nietzsche was not yet five years old, and the family moved to Naumburg, where young Nietzsche grew up in a household consisting of his mother, sister, grandmother, and two maiden aunts. There is every evidence that the child was a model of behavior and a highly talented pupil, whom his playmates called "the little pastor" because of his precocious dignity. At ten he wrote several plays and composed music; Elisabeth claimed the credit for having preserved many proofs of his creative genius which are now part of the Nietzsche Archives she founded at Weimar. His fellow students respected him as much as his teachers. The young Nietzsche showed early a gift for self-analysis—a gift that was to make him later the author of the autobiographical *Ecce Homo*—and wrote his first autobiography at fourteen.

There had always been an apocryphal tradition in the family that the Nietzsches were descendants of Polish aristocracy, and young Friedrich used to sign his name as Nicky, or Friedrich W. v. Nietsky. When the boy once had composed several mazurkas, he dedicated the small collection to the "memory of our ancestors." Reminiscing at the age of thirty-nine, the philosopher wrote of himself proudly as the descendant of Polish aristocrats who had suffered because of their Protestant faith. He referred to his appearance as of the "Polish type," recording proudly how Italians used to speak of him as "il Polacco" and how Polish travellers had frequently mistaken him for one of their fellow countrymen. In Switzerland the German philosopher introduced himself as a Swiss to a Pole, but was again flattered by being considered Polish. But even Elisabeth, who has always defended her brother's peculiarities in a fanatical and unreasonable manner, speaks of these Polish ties as a myth based on little or no reliable information.

The boy submitted himself willingly to the rigorous discipline and academic training of the famous Pforta Boarding School, which he entered at fourteen. Once more it seemed like an ironic touch of history that the study of religion proved to be one of his best subjects there. Pforta demanded of its graduating students a *curriculum vitae,* a brief autobiographical sketch that has been preserved in Nietzsche's case. He speaks of the years from nine to fifteen as the ones characterized by an urge for "universal knowledge" and notes also the doctrinaire zeal with which he used to play and write little "books," submitting them to his friends. Naturally he speaks also about his musical training and comments upon his lack of concentration, a weakness in which Pforta caused him to make some change, although even in 1864, when entering Bonn University, he still felt the need for a more rigid self-discipline. His Pforta teachers called his work in religion, Latin, and German essay-writing outstanding, commending him also on his mastery of German and Greek literature, while criticizing him in several other respects. The graduation certificate speaks of his intention to study classical philology and theology at Bonn University and expresses the hope that he might "achieve in his vocation a level of great efficiency."

Nietzsche soon felt disgusted with the beer-drinking and carousing fraternity life at Bonn, and for some time his letters home continued to reflect the sound moral standards of the family. But his fellow student, Paul Deussen, later an authority in the field of Sanskrit, published in his *Memoirs of Friedrich Nietzsche*, after the philosopher's death, an episode of Nietzsche's student days that is likely to have been a turning point in Nietzsche's moral and spiritual development. Arriving in Cologne one day, Nietzsche asked a guide to show him to a hotel. This sinister character brought him to a house of prostitution, where the inexperienced and confused young man saw in the sad company of women a piano, the only "being" in the room that seemed still to have a soul. Rushing toward it, he played a few chords and then hurried outside. Thomas Mann has expressed the suspicion that he may have returned at some later time, and the author of *Doctor Faustus* uses this episode in his novel, making Nietzsche's double, Leverkuehn, undergo the same traumatic experience. In 1869, Nietzsche reported at the Basel students' clinic that he had contracted syphilis three years earlier, and we know that he had twice been infected.

It is, of course, especially tempting to attach a psychoanalytical significance to these experiences because his later extreme opinions on women and his unfortunate personal fate as a solitary prophet might well have had their roots in such early moral shocks. These theories are all the more plausible as his life was rather uneventful and scarcely supplies the external motivation for his explosive philosophy.

But as in the case of Kierkegaard, a philosopher's spiritual evolution cannot possibly be traced back solely to personal experiences. Nietzsche's enthusiasm for the world of

Greek and Roman antiquity; his interest in contemporary philosophy, especially in Schopenhauer; his enthusiasm for music and his devotion to Wagner, passing as the friendship of the two proved to be; his passionate interest in every phase of artistic and literary life at Bonn and later in Leipzig, together with the turbulent political events of his time, have undoubtedly been the most strongly determining factors in his spiritual evolution. There were three wars in short succession (1864, 1866, and 1870–71), and Nietzsche saw a short period of service as a medical aid in the Franco-Prussian war. Thomas Mann points toward the core of his being when he characterizes him as a tender and sensitive artist in need of affection and not one made to live in the torturing aloneness that was to become his fate.

Such considerations, however, do not necessarily remove the influence of the physical and moral shocks of his student days, from which he must have suffered more intensely than modern medical and psychological progress permit us to comprehend. Nietzsche's violent rebellion against the tables of old and his barbarian display of strength and power can only evoke sympathy for whatever moral pains he experienced. These shocks undoubtedly contributed to his outlook on life. And once he had outgrown the rigid bounds of family tradition and religious training, no inhibition seemed able to control his thinking and keep it within reason. He became a Cyclops hurling devastation and defiance at Europe's society. Nothing was left of his religious background except the extreme contradiction to everything that once had been sacred to him.

His most revered teacher at Bonn University was Friedrich Ritschl, whose research in antiquity determined for at least a whole generation the standards of research in this field; and when Ritschl transferred his university teaching to Leipzig, Nietzsche followed him there. At Leipzig, Nietzsche's best friend was Erwin Rohde, later the famous author of *Psyche;* but this friendship cooled off when

Rohde married, after having established himself as a scholar, and became increasingly critical of Nietzsche's revolutionary zeal. Shortly before the outbreak of Nietzsche's insanity (1889), Rohde said of him, "There was something about him that I had never met before. He was as though he had come from a land where nobody else was living."

Nietzsche's student days came to an abrupt end when he was called to Basel University to teach classical philology even before he had received his doctor's degree. This appointment, a rare distinction for a young man of twenty-four, may well have strengthened his inordinate self-esteem to the excessive degree that has become associated with him.

He taught at Basel for ten years (1869–1879). His persistent illness, partly caused by the strain of his brief service in the Franco-Prussian war, forced his retirement at the age of thirty-five. The story of his physical sufferings is again open to a predominantly psychological analysis. His tantalizing attacks of migraine, his ever-recurring stomach ailments, and the long-lasting periods of weakness, not only paralyzed his creative strength but also aroused in him a rare effort to resist the whims of his body by spiritual energies. In this will to overpower his illness he even came to regard health without an inward spiritual substance as nothing but sickness, whereas an undefeated spiritual existence was only possible in resistance to physical obstacles, of which he had more than his share. His retirement afforded at least leisure for his writing, and his most exciting books were the products of this period of enforced academic inactivity.

Nietzsche's friendship with Richard Wagner rose to the highest point during his Basel period. He not only revered Wagner as an eminent composer but also regarded him as a kind of prophetic apparition in a drab age of mediocrity. Wagner was living proof that true genius is independent of time and circumstance; the composer's hostility to the

Christian faith and his bold revival of Germanic paganism in his operas made a lasting impression upon the young Nietzsche. It is easy to see traces of such influences in Nietzsche's later works, especially in *The Antichrist*. Wagner held Christianity to be alien to Germanic culture and racial instinct; it had Jewish, or oriental, roots. It created nothing but hypocrisy, the negation of the will to power; it would lead to shameful weakness and the ultimate cessation of life. Christianity, so Wagner believed, had "choked off" the artistic impulses of the German nation. Now Wotan was to replace Jehovah, and Siegfried would be the Germanic Christ. Wagner's boastful prediction that "my baton will yet become the scepter of the future" sounded convincing to the music-intoxicated and work-drunk Nietzsche, who also worshipped Wagner's wife Cosima as a modern Greek goddess, speaking of her in his later insane ravings as "my wife Cosima Wagner."

The "magic of extremes," to which Nietzsche was ever so easily surrendering, turned him at last against Richard Wagner, whose folk mania, anti-Semitism, and pompous self-deification repelled Nietzsche more and more, so that he even attacked Wagner publicly in his writings.

There were good reasons on Nietzsche's side for the unfortunate outcome of this friendship, but the human disillusionment was also one more proof of Nietzsche's inability to maintain ties of lasting friendship. This trait interfered in an even more tragic manner in Nietzsche's friendship with Lou Salomé, a young woman of Russian-Finnish background, and a person of unusual intellect, artistic intuition, and personal charm. She seemed destined to fulfill the philosopher's most ardent desire for someone who would not only be an heir to his thoughts but also develop them beyond their present stage. But, again, this friendship came to nothing, although Nietzsche believed for a time that his love for her might find a response. The illusion at one time had even prompted him to propose marriage to her through the mediation of Paul Rée, a common friend of the two, who, however, seems not to have carried out his delicate mission. An abrupt separation followed, and there is reason to believe that Elisabeth Nietzsche, jealous and prejudiced as she proved to be on many other occasions during and after the philosopher's life, had also interfered in this affair.

Nietzsche's literary production began with *The Birth of Tragedy* (1872), an attempt to interpret Greek art and drama in the light of Schopenhauer's philosophy. His *Untimely Meditations* (1873–1876) were in part critical and controversial, but the last two, dedicated to Schopenhauer and Wagner, presented appreciative interpretations of the two great minds. The most decisive break with the thinking of the past occurred during his retirement and the ensuing social isolation. *Human All—Too Human* (1878–1880), *The Dawn of Day* (1881), *The Gay Science* (1882), *Thus Spake Zarathustra* (1882–1885), *Beyond Good and Evil* (1886), *Genealogy of Morals* (1887), *The Twilight of the Idols* (1889), the posthumously published *Antichrist,* and his final spiritual self-characterization, *Ecce Homo,* are part and parcel of his gigantic "revaluation of all values," marking various stages in this spiritual revolution. His *Will to Power,* the "history of the next two centuries" published after his death, had not been completed in systematic form.

Much of these later writings evolved in ecstatic states of mind and were written with the furious speed that reminds one of Kierkegaard's creative energy. Their unsystematic character is only in part explained by his illness and the high tension characteristic of his work methods. He seemed unable to channel the never ending flow of new thoughts and fleeting visions into an ordered literary form, a manner he rejected anyway as part of a dying era. His thoughts on the nature of man, religion, politics, music, and art are scattered over many of his writings and only grow into coherent unity when viewed within the total design of his thinking. He was aware of the nature of his presentation; but again and again the alchemy of his brilliant language added its own seductive charm to his nervous tendency, and he surrendered as often to the temptation of playing with words as with ideas.

Though he had been an outsider at Basel University, during the years of his retirement he became even more lonely than before. He conceived many of his literary ideas during his excursions in the mountains, his frequent visits to Northern Italy, and in endless solitary broodings in his room. The fight against his illness, the true nature of which is likely to remain unknown, caused depressing periods of melancholy, which alternated with manic states of elation and pride. Many a time he expected death to overcome him.

He wrote, "It is a crucial fact that the spirit prefers to descend upon the sick and suffering." His various references to sickness as a "great stimulant" having the function of hardening him and spurring the creative impulses are quite characteristic of the stoicism which he demanded for facing life's vicissitudes without the aid of Christian religion. Towards the end the torments of his illness accelerated his mental excesses; there were no more restraints in his thinking, and the meteoric fire of his earlier grandiose ideas dissolved in little sparks and ashes. He attacked everything and everybody in unbridled lust for destruction and nihilism, exalting himself to the rank of a deity and world ruler. "How to Philosophize with a Hammer," the subtitle of his *Will to Power,* was symbolical of this entire final phase. He had, indeed, become the "dynamite" which he had called himself in his autobiographical *Ecce Homo,* a book containing such chapters as "Why I Am So Intelligent," "Why I Write Such Good Books," "Why I Am Fate." He spoke of himself as the "Successor to the dead God," "Nietzsche-Caesar," "The Crucified One," and "Dionysius." He decreed that Emperor Wilhelm should be placed before a court and executed. Insanity was clearly overpowering a mind that had formerly been so brilliant.

Medical opinions about his illness have always been divided, but the syphilitic infection and subsequent paresis are likely to have been among the determining factors in his breakdown. The end came while he was in Turin, the very city where lived Cesare Lombroso, psychiatrist and author of the widely known *Genius and Insanity*. Nietzsche collapsed in the street and had to be taken to Basel and later to a Jena asylum.

The pictures of his childhood and youth convey the impression of unusual intelligence and alertness, as do his photographs taken in 1867 and 1882, when he was at the height of his creative period. In contrast to these, Nietzsche's photograph as a sword-bearing, private, first-class artilleryman, taken in 1868, is as grotesque as his repeated boasts that his intellectual attacks had the force of artillery fire. Hans Olde's last etching of the sick philosopher, taken shortly before his death, still retains some distant suggestion of the grandeur which Max Klinger has bestowed upon his idealized marble statue, but it is, nevertheless, a sad image of decay and derangement. The volcanic glow of the eyes has disappeared, and the anxious letters of his mother speak of hours and days on end during which the patient, while gazing into empty space, uttered not a single word.

Nietzsche died in 1900. He is buried in the churchyard at Roecken, where his father had baptized him and where a strictly Lutheran tradition on both sides of the family had seemed to assure the formation of a Christian character. But it was Nietzsche's fate to regard himself as an "atheist by instinct" and to become Europe's most prominent nihilist. Humanity has yet been spared the "universal madness" which he predicted for the moment when mankind would discover that there is no God. The frightful doom of this vision was to be the tragic fate of the philosopher himself.

Chapter 2

As SUGGESTED EARLIER, Nietzsche's thoughts do not come to us in neat packages of systematic thinking. We are close to a fire when we listen to him, sensing both the consuming heat and the blinding light of his spirit. Like Kierkegaard, he demands of us passion and exaltation, and he will be understood only when we surrender to the magic fireworks of his extremes and contradictions. He creates a mood rather than a rational conviction, and it is no surprise that he has been favorably quoted by believers as well as atheists, by conservatives as well as rebels. For almost every one of his truths there can be found another truth contradicting the first. The subtitle of *Thus Spake Zarathustra* indicates this inherent contradiction: it is "a book for everybody and nobody."

Much of his thinking is a monologue, a persistent contradiction within himself, which ends at last in the exclusive self-reflections of *Ecce Homo,* written shortly before the outbreak of his insanity. "I have been more of a battlefield than a man," he said. His thinking is one great protest against the logical construction of a philosophical system, an explosive trend that had begun with Kierkegaard's rebellion against a "system about being which cannot possibly exist." He has his own tragic share of the tensions between reason and instinct, emotion and logic, tradition and irreverence so characteristic of his time, that were to foreshadow the breakdown of Europe's civilization. He wants to be an artist, a prophet or saint, and a teacher, but he is again and again fascinated by exalted visions and images that defy systematic presentation. His thinking is the product of emotional sensation which gives his entire work a chaotic as well as an artistic note. Any noble thought rising in him is immediately attacked by rebellious, brilliant, or cynical counter arguments and suspicion. He knows he can never find his true self; it must remain elusive, tragically hidden. But instead of regretting this condition, he praises error as a basic element of life, to be accepted heroically. Everybody and everything must grow in opposition to resistance, contradiction, darkness, and death.

Nietzsche consciously employed the methods of indirect communication which had also been Kierkegaard's enigmatic tool. Instead of speaking himself, he makes Zarathustra speak, or the "free spirit," and many of Nietzsche's extreme statements are meant to produce agreement as well as opposition or the divining of a half truth. They initiate chain reactions of intuitive perspectives. The pseudo-scriptural language in which *Zarathustra* is written sets the mood for a receptive reverence, only to be shattered at the will of the prophet. Much of it is an appeal, a question, an ambiguity, or a seeming play on words. As in the case of Kierkegaard, truth is for Nietzsche too profound, elusive, and vast to be caught in bare words. It is of the essence of life itself; and silence, the mask of gaiety and lightmindedness, the ironic wisdom of the jester and buffoon, or man's double, are necessary for conveying some of the dialectical character of truth. His judgments are more than appraisals of that which is; their volatile and propelling force has the power of transcendence. When he seems to deal with the past or present, the invisible hand of his magic language removes barriers to the future and new perspectives suddenly open up.

Kierkegaard's key word is "spirit." Nietzsche's emphasis was on life, power, and instinct, all threatened by intellect and spirit, perverted by a misfit culture, and to be defended by an undefinable vitalism. In spite of the tragic seriousness of his life and his later influence upon politics, there has always been something Quixotic about Nietzsche's claim that he was a reformer or revolutionist, and it is interesting to read of his intense interest in the figure of Don Quixote de la Mancha. Like him, Nietzsche lived most of his life in a void. His friendships were few and short-lived; his career as a university teacher was all too brief. He was a master artist in the realm of theory, meditation, and dream, but not a man of action, neither in life nor death fitted for the tragic role in Europe's disintegration which he was destined to play after his death.

As in all existentialist thinking, his true realm was the future, the potential, and his perceptive medium was a sensitive intuition. That which existed or appeared as the fleeting essence of life was unsupported, fragile, and fraught with peril. He spoke of himself as the "philosopher of the hazardous 'perhaps.' " Life's motion forward and upward was to him the beautiful urge worthy of the artist's senses.

Much as his brilliant intellectual universalism impresses us, his passion remained within Kierkegaard's "first stage," the aesthetic. It is rather significant that his friends and foes agree only on his poetry's undisputed perfection. His attacks upon morality and the middle class move him close to Oscar Wilde's degenerative aestheticism, although Nietzsche's image of the coming man appeared austere and heroic. His borderless prophecies were no substitute for the morality he set out to destroy in his fury for creating chaos. His frontier thinking lacked the essence of concrete guidance toward a realizable goal. The lonely philosopher's desire to remain a Single One was part of his self-chosen destiny, and he could promise nothing but a solitary and mysterious nobility to man when he should succeed in becoming what he was meant to be.

Like Kierkegaard and Tolstoy, Nietzsche neither expects nor wants to find disciples. He wants new "single ones" at a time when the average mass man no longer counts.

His own unhappy experiences undoubtedly colored his views on man. There is a mixture of pity, love, and condescension in his image of man: man is a cruel, courageous, and vain animal. He is "God's monkey," whom God in His long eternities created for a pastime. But man is also aware of values of which no animal knows anything. Yet man, the blond beast, cannot trust himself. He takes out his resentments on others when plagued by dissatisfaction with himself. He is vain, oversensitive, resentful, proud, and, of course, dishonest with himself. Everything in human conduct can be reduced to the will for self-assertion. Much of Freud's and Adler's later thinking had been anticipated by Nietzsche in an intuitive manner that makes these psychologists everlastingly indebted to him.

The truly valuable beings are artists, philosophers, and perhaps also the saints. But the superman is destined to fulfill our highest dreams. Nietzsche's vision was that of the new man, the one who not only will reproduce himself but build himself up to a being beyond the "much-too-many," the mob. He will be a higher but, of course, also a lonely man. The time is drawing to a close when it was enough to be merely a contemporary, one of the crowd. The future man is needed, the superman, whom society will not yet recognize and to whom it will attach the stigma of loneliness. His secret nobility will be of an aristocratic elevation, for which no pattern exists: he has nobody to follow, and nobody should be asked to follow him. If he should ever step before the public with a claim for superiority, he will soon become dishonest, attempt a selfish rule, and like Napoleon, degenerate into a despicable and dangerous beast.

Nietzsche's judgments about his fellow men are, however, something other than venomous insults. At the bottom of his heart he loves man, but wants him to become better, higher, nobler than he cares to be himself. Man's dishonesty with himself is his greatest enemy. When he makes a mistake, his memory admits, "I have done this," but his pride opposes by saying, "I cannot have done this," and pride wins out over memory. Man, according to Nietzsche, is full of contradictions, loves life, creative work, splendor, success, and, of course, he loves himself; but he also cherishes a secret love for the nothing, for annihilation, and destruction.

Much of this image is, naturally, a reflection of Nietzsche's thinking about himself. He suffers so much from the split in his whole being that he speaks of himself at one and the same time as of a beginning and an end. He is a beginning, meaning an entirely new type of man, who belongs to a different astronomical order of the spirit and whose message will be a landmark in history; he "breaks mankind's history into two pieces." But he considers himself also decadent, the first European nihilist who denies all existing values. He is at once destroyer and builder, and in this regard his gospel is of one piece. It is, therefore, only logical when he asks us not to read his books "like looting soldiers," choosing appealing passages at random from his aphorisms (which he was the first to employ extensively in German literature); instead, we are to read ourselves into "a passionate mood" in order to perceive the short rays of light that will lead us onward and upward. He is fully aware that his teachings are meant for only the few; yet he feels the duty to speak out publicly in the marketplace, because he hopes inaudible echoes will arise in the few who may feel the appeal.

Thus Nietzsche's work aims at being an appeal, a new gospel, but not a system of philosophy. Nietzsche's *Zarathustra* has probably had the most far-reaching influence in Europe. It was said that the two books which thousands of German soldiers carried during the First World War were the New Testament and *Zarathustra*. Subsequent events in the rise of Hitlerism, with its emphasis on racial superiority, have shown many traces of *Zarathustra's* influence. Yet it would be incorrect to call this book his chief work. There is no *magnum opus* of Nietzsche. All his books are the volcanic testimonies of a genius whose burning passion to see the new man rising was unable to channel his lightning-like thoughts into the calm language of reason or the methodical persuasion of the teacher. He was a prophet, chosen and doomed, knowing, like Kierkegaard, that only a few "single ones" might be kindled by his spark, yet having to address the same wide audience whom he thought he had to condemn. And again like Kierkegaard, he was surrounded by mediocrity, exposed to the censorship of misunderstanding and ill-will, and forced to finance many of his publications, now treasured as a part of world literature.

Nietzsche's pessimistic image of man as a slave to himself and others, by implication and in open combat, attacks man's moral principles. The new "superman," a term taken from Goethe's *Faust,* is law unto himself. He is autonomous and will impose his wishes upon the "much-too-many," those of whom Melville's Ahab in *Moby Dick* had spoken over thirty years earlier (1851) as "a mob of unnecessary duplicates."

The clever device of these "superfluous ones" is to subject the great and free man to their own "slave morality" by adopting Jesus' teachings of humility, meekness, and suffering. They follow a "pale, anemic" Christian ideal, by which they judge everyone. A Christian's thinking is perverted; even when he humbles himself, he does so only to be exalted (in contradiction of Luke XVIII: 14). His great delight is the mean and petty pleasure of condemning others. Society, considering itself moral and good in the conventional, Christian sense, hates the higher type of man and considers his isolation the result of guilt and the well deserved stigma of social unfitness. The morality it wants is nothing more than to reduce everyone to its own level; man as a Christian occupies proudly the judgment seat. But Jesus, for whom Nietzsche always preserves a high regard, was not a judge. Nietzsche emphasizes the fact that Jesus opposed those who judged others, and wanted to destroy the morality existing in his age. Christ's rebellion attacked the Jewish hierarchy, the "just" and supreme rulers, and Nietzsche calls him an anarchist who had to die for this sin, not for the sins of others. Jesus abolished the idea of guilt and sin. How could he have died for the sins of others?

God, like life itself, is beyond and above good and evil. Christ's morality was fit to be lived only by Christ himself, a thought akin to that of Dostoevsky's Grand Inquisitor, who also reserves Christ's morality to a few thousand supermen. Jesus remains the only Christian who ever lived —but he was crucified by man. The Christians are making of their professed faith a weird comedy. Jewish-Christian morality is "the instinct of the herd against the strong and independent ones," an instinct also against the happy ones who are creators of their own law. Christian morality is the child of resentment and confesses its own inability to know what is good or bad; it teaches that God alone has this knowledge.

But God has died!

Chapter 3

NIETZSCHE CALLS THIS change in our thinking the greatest "event" of our time. The new knowledge that faith in God has become impossible and is no longer worthy of acceptance is equivalent to the setting of the sun. Now the world appears to those realizing this "event" somehow older, strange, and suspicious; we are living at a late hour of mankind. The post-Christian era has begun. Nobody knows what the results of this "event" will be. Everything will collapse that was built upon his past faith in God, as, for example, our entire European morality. An appalling sequence of terrors will logically ensue. Only the few select ones, those who actually should belong to the coming centuries but were prematurely born, the riddle-solvers, who are living on mountain tops to get a glimpse of future knowledge—these will sense the light, happiness, encouragement, and the sunrise of the new day. Their hearts will overflow with gratitude, astonishment, and expectancy. Their ships may sail again toward unknown shores. The daring search for new knowledge is once more permitted; the seas lie open before them. Perhaps there was never before such an "open ocean."

God has died!

This terrifying proclamation rallies all energies in Nietzsche to a final attack upon the sacred beliefs of Christianity. He respects, or even admires Jesus, but denies that he has any meaning for our age. "When we hear on a Sunday morning our old bells ringing, we ask ourselves, 'Is this possible? This is still being done for a Jew crucified 2,000 years ago, who told us he was the son of God.'" Our religion is a piece of antiquity transposed into modern times. We are made to believe "in a God who has a child with a mortal woman; a sage who demands that we discontinue to work or maintain courts of justice, and who tells us that the most important task is to watch the signs of the coming end of the world . . . he requests of his disciples to drink his blood. . . ." "Is it possible that such things are still being believed?"

In the vein of Kierkegaard's thinking, with which he was unacquainted, Nietzsche, the Antichrist, is indignant about the unholy fusion of state and religion, as he also believes that the state prevents the Single One from attaining his dignity. Original Christianity taught man not to conform to the state and even to separate himself from his family for the sake of the spirit. Our statesmen, "anti-Christians in their deeds," have clearly changed this. They attend communion. They promote "Christian" thinking in their speeches and schools. The chasm between the world and the faith of Jesus has been eliminated. Now the Christian is a soldier, a judge, a patriot who knows nothing about non-resistance to evil. He defends his honor instead of accepting humiliations; he is as proud as though he had never heard of the humble Galilean's teachings, and the Church has become precisely that institution Jesus had wanted to abolish.

Nietzsche's brilliant and poetic style serves to give his denial of Jesus' mission an effective literary background: "Only a Jewish setting could have produced Jesus. I mean a landscape overhung by the dark majestic thunderclouds of Jehovah. Only here could one sense as a miracle of 'love' the rare and sudden breaking of a single sun ray through the all-pervasive twilight, a ray of unmerited 'grace.' Only here could Christ dream of his rainbows, his ladder toward heaven upon which God descended to man. Anywhere else the sun and bright weather were too much part of every day's normal rule." No, modern man can no longer accept Jesus' teachings. He will stoically face his fate and wrestle with adversities. He needs no longer the priests who have done nothing but to "anesthetize human evil" instead of strengthening man to face it. The result is that the ordinary Christian is a miserable figure who does not really deserve the harsh punishment with which Christianity threatens him in afterlife. Christianity has created sin, this sickness of the soul, but the belief in Christianity's remedies is rapidly waning. The Churches are nothing but graves and gravestones of God, and "the Christian resolve to consider the world ugly and bad has made the world just that."

Nietzsche's hatred of Christian morality extends to the Jewish race. He says, "Sin is a Jewish sentiment and a Jewish invention." Such damning verdicts are, however, contradicted by an occasional fair appraisal of the Jewish people. He realizes that their accumulated capital in intellect and will power, the result of generations of suffering and persecution, has made them hated everywhere. Yet he also praises them for having produced in Jesus the "noblest man," in Spinoza the purest sage, and in the Bible the most effective moral code in the world.

Then he turns with renewed force against Christianity. He calls it the religion of compassion, a depressing sentiment that saps our vitality. Compassion annihilates the high tone of life; it leads to weakness, and is the practice of nihilism. The Christian God is a God of the sick, one who opposes all the natural and impetuous urges of great living. No wonder that a true Christian is a "physiological degenerate." There is only one aristocratic figure in the New Testament: Pontius Pilate. His disdainful question, "What is truth?" (meaning, of course, that truth does not count in the world of realities), is the only word of lasting value in the New Testament. (It is only logical that Nietzsche's disciple, Oswald Spengler, speaks of this same question as "the only New Testament word that has any racial quality.") The strong races of North Europe have been deprived of their vigor by this Christian God; they have become sick and old, incapable of a new religious concept. Almost two thousand years have gone by, and not a single new God has come to us! Christianity has soiled and spoiled everything, created a false equality, and paralyzed our vital energies with the anemic ideal of hypocritical saintliness. The laws of life are high above Christian idealism.

Nietzsche accuses the Church of having perverted man's attitude toward sex, his most Olympian and powerful instinct. Eternal damnation has always been so closely associated with sexual matters that the very term sin has become a synonym for sex. Whole generations of Christians have been reproducing themselves with a guilty conscience. That is, incidentally, the reason the love story is the most popular medium for man's imaginative and escapist tendencies. The waste of spiritual energies in Christianity is appalling; our Churches have employed the fear techniques of a decaying civilization in order to stir up man's nervous energies; they make him feel sinful.

Nietzsche's criticism of missionary work is equally severe. In reality, the Christian Church is, so he suggests, nothing but a collection of primitive and predatory cults and beliefs. "Not the essentially Christian, but the universally pagan of its ceremonies (the last supper) is the reason for its expansion." Wherever the missionary has gone, the Church has adapted itself to existing superstitions and practices; while this technique may appear a skilful method to win over pagans, it illustrates clearly the coarseness and baseness of its intellectual status. Primitive tribes accept the two European narcotics, whiskey and Christianity, most willingly. They have also declined most quickly from these two causes.

Such a basically unheroic and insincere Church was, and is, of course, too far gone to be improved or reformed. The Reformation was nothing but the paralyzing of half of Christianity's body. It was treason of the meanest kind to revive a Church that showed all the marks of decay. When Luther came, with his perverting theology of justification by faith, Europe had already begun to rise again from the coma which the Christian poison had induced. The Renaissance promised an almost miraculous revival of the arts and sciences in their natural vitality, and in Rome, the very seat of the dying Church, the new life rose as a strong youth rises besides his aging ancestor.

There could have been hardly any doubt about the outcome of this development if Luther had not come. A Cesare Borgia would have been the man to finish off a corrupt and dying Christianity, but Luther came, this misfit priest, full of vindictive instincts, and intent on leading a peasant revolt against the Renaissance. To his own consternation he saw that the corrupt papacy was no longer in power, but that the great "Yes" to life was being spoken by the revived antiquity of the Renaissance.

The clumsy Germans destroyed the Renaissance as they have always destroyed every other great freedom. "They are my enemies," and their filthy hands left nothing untouched. Their conscience is burdened with the creation of Protestantism, the most incurable sickness of Europe. The poet, Stefan George, his disciple and the leader of the George Kreis, expressed the same thought in his cycle, *The Seventh Ring,* when he praised the Renaissance as an awakening with clouds of flowers drifting into the country, which the ugly frost of quarrel and dogmatism chased away.

Luther's robust mind, so Nietzsche says in *The Gay Science,* had no understanding of the Mediterranean sense of freedom of the spirit and the Mediterranean sense of mistrust for and suspicion of nature, man, and the spirit. He did not understand the victory of the Church but saw only its corruption, not realizing the aristocratic skepticism and tolerance which any victorious power will permit. He delivered the sacred Book into everybody's hands, including the scholars', who have always been destroyers of faith. Kierkegaard, the Protestant, raised the same accusation against Luther when he said, "He threw the Bible at their (the believers') heads." Luther allowed the priests freedom of sex without realizing that the faith of three-fourths of the people, especially that of the women, rested upon the exceptional position the priests held in not being subject to the physical laws of life. Nor did he realize that the faith in miracles had its roots in the same admiration of the priestly celibacy which he abolished. Once he had taken this step, he had logically also to abolish confession, that "discreet cistern and tomb of all secrets," which the priest was meant to represent.

Luther thus abolished a higher type of man because he hated him. He ought not to be held responsible, however, for the appalling superficialities which Protestantism developed later on, for he did not realize what forces he had set in motion. But he marks the victory of mediocrity, philistinism, and a mob psychology that is the end of all true spiritual grandeur.

About 1870, in the midst of ascending political power and increasing prosperity, Nietzsche had sensed the first signs of Europe's intellectual and spiritual sterility. "We shall either die because of our religion, or religion will die because of us," he wrote. And about ten years later he diagnosed his age as one lacking authority, fear, and trust. Everything was being dissolved in idle palaver. Germany's victory over France and the newly created empire had produced a shallow self-confidence and a brazen sense of superiority that were ultimately to lead to new catastrophes.

The Bismarck era saw an unexcelled boom, the mushrooming of new business enterprises, and a subsequent orgy of public and private building of inferior taste. Nietzsche realized that the traditional confidence in religion was quickly giving way to an unlimited faith in scientific progress, to which Germany was one of the leading contributors. The soul of the nation aspired only to security, prosperity, and a kind of "eternal bliss," inferior to the promises of religion. This was, emphatically, the end of the much vaunted idealism of Kant and Schiller and even of the altruistic patriotism of poets like Arndt and Koerner. Only the most concrete and crude goals remained; man was unashamedly revealing himself as the beast he was. He was rebelling against all higher values, and this rebellion killed God, because "He has witnessed the depths and abysses of man, all his hidden meanness and ugliness.

. . . Man cannot bear to have a witness!" God was a danger to man's self-appointed rule and therefore had to die. Now that He is dead, man is confronted by an ocean of uncertainty, an infinity of nothingness, a situation of apocalyptic character.

These keen diagnostic extremes are accompanied by only a distant regret. While Nietzsche deplores the absence of reverence, trust, fear, and idealism, he makes the general decay an occasion for a personal rebellion and the usurping of divine rank: "If there were any gods, how could I bear not to be one! Therefore, there are no gods!"

Chapter 4

ONCE HE HAS taken this step, Nietzsche assumes the Herculean task of sweeping away all the cherished traditions of European thinking. He examines the meaning of history, politics, war, revolutions, human rights, education, and the ultimate meaning of life and death. The sluice gates are open, and there are no inhibitions to his destructive attacks. Nothing can bar him any longer from weighing the old values and destroying the sacred tables in the entire field of civilization.

He, the admirer of Greek antiquity, feels no restraint before history; the revolutionist is always ahistorical. It had become an accepted philosophical principle that history was God's own handiwork. The historian Ranke had solemnly stated that every nation was a specific thought of God's creative will, but Nietzsche saw in history nothing but a succession of events without underlying laws. Schopenhauer had defined the world and its forces as manifestations of the will to power, but Nietzsche did not hesitate to declare history "brutal and senseless." Hegel's optimistic idea that man's history is an ascending design of progress he held to be absurd. Man as a species has not made progress; our general education and democracy have merely smothered the influence of the truly Single Ones who carried the burden of progress. From now on the "breeding" of a better, higher, and more aristocratic type must be the aim of education. So Nietzsche wrote seventy years ago, in a style very similar to that of Dostoevsky's Grand Inquisitor and the conspirators in *The Possessed*. Only forty to fifty years were to elapse before Europe was to witness in the triumph of dictatorships in Russia, Italy, and Germany, that man is anxious to kneel down in submission before anyone with the real will to power.

The new commanders must have the strength to live without God. They will also have to renounce all happiness since they are going to be lonely men. While imposing their will upon the people, they are, nevertheless, dependent on them, but will at the same time continue to live in aristocratic detachment and aloneness. The military relationship between officer and man will have to serve as a model for the future leader. Both are linked together by a higher ideal, whereas the present industrialist and his workers are nothing but opposing rivals without a common goal. The industrialist as a money-maker cannot belong to a higher race. The future nation will give an honorarium to the worker, not wages. The state will rule everybody's thinking; it will become the new "idol."

Chapter 5

NIETZSCHE'S LAST WRITINGS during the eighties develop vast schemes of world prophecy.

From now on only great politics will count. National politics such as had dominated German thinking (and, in spite of himself, also Nietzsche's) would soon be a matter of the past. There will be a United Europe as Napoleon had envisioned it. A decade earlier Nietzsche had already spoken of the coming European League of Nations and the need for the organization of a global world economy. An era of several centuries had begun in which the one big problem will be the rule over the entire world, and "there will be wars such as they have never been." Wars are part of the very nature of a state, and although he did not want to glorify wars for their own sake, Nietzsche considered them revivers of national strength. He also said that society is "a means toward wars." In a way that is quite similar to Dostoevsky's nihilistic visions, Nietzsche foresaw a period of chaos, of untamed and "entirely merciless forces." "The masses will rule, the individual has to lie in order to belong to the masses." Barbarism and a fantastic energy will appear together with the despotism of the state. "Everything will be mob rule . . ." "the atheists, immoralists, libertines of all kinds, artists, Jews, and gamblers." But the truly strong ones will quietly wait, observe, and then fight wars such as there have never been in mankind's earlier history.

The United States, of which Nietzsche had only a most superficial knowledge derived exclusively from reading, is only "seemingly" a world power. She will be "quickly consumed." Dostoevsky had prophesied in 1864 that the English would eventually abandon their island and that "our grandsons" will "witness the exodus of the English from Europe." Nietzsche, in a similar manner gave England only another fifty years to last as a world power.

The powers to count in this coming struggle are Germany and particularly Russia. The most momentous event of the future will be Russia's appearance as a world power and force in shaping civilization. As yet this vast country was barbarian. But the Russians can wait. Their art, the magnanimity of their youth, and their "fantastic insanity" (*sic*) will be irresistible. "Russia must become the ruler over Europe and Asia; she must colonize and win over China and India." Russia "can bide her time" and follow the principle to proceed "as slowly as possible." For a time Nietzsche shared with many politicians the hope that Germany and Russia might become allies.

But then, as though dark fears were overcoming him, he also saw the need for a united Europe to resist Russia. Whatever structure was to evolve, nothing would be lasting. The future would be incalculable, bottomless, uncertain. Our historians are nothing but the pawnbrokers of the past. They are always subservient to present powers and prove gladly that the current régime is right. In his low opinion of historians he corroborated the dictum of Edgar Quinet, who in 1875 wrote in his *L'esprit nouveau,* "There is nothing so corrupt as history when it enters the servitude (of the state)." Lasting peace will come, not because some weak-kneed pacifists will be successful in persuading us that disarmament is the safest way to peace but because the strong and victorious ones will voluntarily forego their claim to domination and "break their swords of their own free will." A party of peace-lovers will be the guarantors of world harmony, true aristocrats who will not defend themselves and not appeal to courts for arbitration. "The true war glories can be felled only by a sudden stroke of lightning, but lightning comes from above."

Yet for generations to come the impulse to fight is important and should be preserved. It is true that war causes the conqueror to become stupid and makes the conquered mean; it also tends to make the peoples barbarous. But war also makes them more "natural," and they will emerge from this "winter" of civilization with more strength for good and evil. A nation that forgets how to die is senile. In war the individual does not count. Life must not be rated high; victory is all.

Nietzsche also ventured to express his vision of some of the disturbing social changes to come. He seems to accept some of Karl Marx's criticism of ruling society without making a sound appraisal of underlying forces and factors. He predicted in rather sweeping terms that there would be only the haves and the have-nots. Civilization, or culture, would be no force in this coming struggle; what it might seem to achieve would be at the same time the beginning of its decay. The people (meaning the masses) want nothing but entertainment and amusement, and the culture of the possessing classes was too shallow and cowardly to save the situation. In fact, the rich would be as eager as the present class of the poor to become socialists if they should find themselves suddenly dispossessed. Society as it exists by the accumulation of wealth is not the result of needs that have been overcome but of greed and a "terrible impatience." All roads should have been kept open to permit a modest prosperity for the small middle classes.

Socialism will mean the end of progress. The Socialists will bring about nothing but general indolence. They ignore the basic inequality of man, and the inevitable outcome of a revolution will be a boring mediocrity and the tyranny of stupid men; there will be a flock without a shepherd. Socialism is nothing but an ill-applied and misunderstood Christian ideal. It will annihilate all individuality and can be maintained only by force and terrorism because it demands a power for the state such as only despotic rulers possess. Democracy is a sort of quarantine against the pest of tyrannical ambitions. Democratic institutions are quite useful but also quite boring.

Chapter 6

THE ABOVE ACCOUNT may briefly characterize Nietzsche's world picture without reflecting his frequently fascinating visions. There are many obvious contradictions. His feverish hands are offering us, as it were, several truths, and he remains as much of a riddle to us as he admittedly was to himself.

The prophetic image of the superman is the counterpoint in all his works, giving them meaning and unity. It is a popular error to interpret this superman only as the blond beast and ruthless tyrant, although it is, again, easy to support such an opinion. The noble type of the superman is aristocratic, silent, and reserved. His road is the *via eminentia*. He suffers from the common misunderstanding that is his lot. This highest, divine type of man is Dionysian, an exalted Grecian type. He revels in the unexcelled joy of living in the sensual pleasure of love, wine, song, springtime, victory over the enemy, and in religious ecstasies. Nietzsche believed for a time that Richard Wagner's work was an expression of this unending exaltation.

Unending?

Nietzsche cannot answer his own question on the meaning of life. It is unanswerable because we are in life, and life holds sway over us. A judgment about the value of life will not be attempted by the strong ones, who are identical with the happy ones. Only those who are sinking down and drowning, the tired ones, are apt to turn to such introspective problems because they have not mastered the art of living in victory, heroism, and beauty. The strong will guard even in times of misfortune the "pathos of distance," bear illness and poverty with equanimity of spirit, and be generous in forgiving those who have harmed them. They show no traces of suspicion and make it their vocation to live in danger.

Chapter 7

THERE REMAINS a last question to consider: What is the meaning of death?

Nietzsche's thinking reveals its dual and contradictory character at this point with tragic finality. He preaches the transcendence of man beyond himself in the superman and even the transcendence of Christianity in something super-Christian. The Christian belief in a life after death has reduced life's value on earth. Man has put his hope in the future instead of perfecting himself here and now. Death is final, and nothing follows it. He does away with man's awe before the great infinity of death. The strong man will want to live in such a way that "he has also the will to die at the right moment." Only life matters; it is absolute, whereas death is irrelevant. Christianity has made of death nothing but a gruesome comedy, a perversion of all values. In the Christian hereafter the healthy and strong ones are punished, while inhibited, slavish ones receive the ample fulfillment of bliss because they have repressed their best natural impulses in life. They have lived in fear of life, anxious to attain heaven. But the strong one never feared life even when it left him "like an unfaithful woman." The fear of death is a "European disease" identical with the fear of hell. It weakens the will to live fully and in exaltation.

Even death, then, must not be permitted to have its own way. The truly creative man wants to die when his ever-rising vision ceases to grow. The sick patient is a parasite for whom it is "indecent" to go on living, and he ought to free others from his sad plight. The "much-too-many" ought to be told that they are a burden to others. The creative superman will know when to die voluntarily. Suicide, therefore, becomes a sacramental and unselfish act.

Chapter 8

THESE "ANSWERS" to the meaning of life and death reveal that Nietzsche is a nihilist. His own definition of this type of thinker is hardly acceptable; he says, "A nihilist is one who judges of the world as it exists that it should not be, whereas he says of the world as it ought to be that it does not exist." But such clever juggling applies equally to the idealist who is disappointed by existing imperfections. It is probably more accurate to call a man a nihilist who considers life meaningless, without moral law, devoid of values common to all men, and without the prospect of a hereafter. Such, too, was Arkady's boastful nihilism in Turgeniev's *Fathers and Sons,* recognizing only as the law that there must be no law. Nietzsche rejects this nihilism as decadent; it is part of Europe's declining mentality. He considered it his mission to "transvalue" all existing values, create new ones, and lead beyond the present good and evil.

Yet his prophetic and frequently striking thoughts have remained negative, vacuous, and without a concrete goal. The most sympathetic student of Nietzsche will sense only a superhuman attempt to rise above the realities of time, tradition, and the world as Nietzsche saw it, a vain Daedalus flight towards the sun. Irrespective of the truth of many of his criticisms, the tragedy of his own life and the even more disastrous consequences of his philosophy for German and European history have assigned him the role of a great destroyer.

Chapter 9

THE RESPONSE TO Nietzsche's work during his life was so weak and sporadic that he had to finance some of his later publications, but already during his last conscious years and even more in the decade following (1890–1900), his reputation spread fairly rapidly. The Danish literary critic, George Brandes, a Jew, who had also helped to revive the memory of the almost forgotten Kierkegaard, claims the merit of having established the philosopher's literary reputation. A growing school of German and French authors began to write articles and books about him. When one reads the subtitles of some of his books, one has to admit that Nietzsche's predictions about his future mission contained more truth than good taste. Europe quickly bestowed upon him the rank of one of mankind's leading thinkers and destroyers.

His pessimistic disbelief in mankind's ability to understand his message and his compensatory pride had been expressed in the subtitles and comments. He had called *Thus Spake Zarathustra* "a book for everybody and nobody." Of his *Antichrist* he had said, "This book belongs to the very few; perhaps no one of them is alive yet"; it was a book for "predestined readers." *Ecce Homo*, that solitary confessional monologue of which he said, "And thus I recount my life to myself," became the object of research and a weird human interest. The thoughts put down in *The Will to Power* were to be "the next two centuries' history." *The Dawn of the Idols* he had called "a small piece but a big declaration of war." It was always the few, the unknown, or those yet to come whom he wanted to address; the rest was "nothing but humanity," deserving to be ignored or despised.

These few were soon to increase by leaps and bounds, a

fact that does not necessarily mean that Nietzsche was always interpreted in the manner he had desired. Europe's spiritual crisis before World War I is hardly better illustrated than by this rapidly spreading Nietzsche cult. His uncanny psychological insight paved the way for modern psychoanalysis as much as Dostoevsky's contributions had done. His denunciations of Church, religion, and morality intensified the existing crisis of faith, especially in Germany.

The deposition of God is a secret deed committed in the darkness of man's mind and always succeeded by the enthronement of a new god. Nietzsche's open proclamation that God had died stirred thousands who from guilt or doubt had remained silent about their unbelief and were now to find a new idol in the superman of varying interpretations. Darwinism, liberalism, higher criticism, and the movement of the socialistic free-thinkers had been feeding their several varieties of skepticism or atheism into this cauldron of rebellion. Nietzsche's political vagaries fascinated the gentle anarchists as well as nihilists, pan-Germanistic dreamers as well as the socialists who were eagerly looking for signs of decomposition or sterility in the ruling classes, and the intelligentsia who were just beginning to get tired of Ibsen. The lonely philosopher's dreams satisfied the romantic notions of those who wanted to live in a pseudo-mystical aristocracy, a sentiment present in unanchored idealists, in youth, and even among pessimists who regarded the rest of humanity as incurably corrupt. The un-German elegance of his style and the daring brilliance of his imagery held an enormous artistic appeal also for French intellectuals. Nietzsche aroused the enthusiasm of the libertine d'Annunzio in Italy and found apostles in England, where even George Bernard Shaw flirted for a time with his mental excesses.

The lack of success during his own lifetime was a strong factor in raising him quickly to the pedestal of martyrdom and prophecy for the many in German and European society who were suffering from grievances and who, like him, had remained frustrated or unassimilated. The fin-de-siècle mood of the nineties ignored the calendar and lived on side by side with aggressive German imperialism. Thousands were longing for the teacher of the abundant life and the new seer.

His universalism allowed anyone of this strange company to find in his message either a complete gospel for the future or at least some nuggets of brilliant insight that were to become priceless treasures in the midst of confusion or spiritual poverty. Nietzsche articulated the hidden sentiments of academic youth more boldly than any other contemporary. He became a cult.

His immediate influence upon German political thought before the First World War was negligible. German tradition supplied an abundance of historians, philosophers, and poets to inspire militarism and nationalism. It was a moot point, anyway, whether he had preached aggression and physical delight in destruction or an aristocratic, spiritual detachment unsoiled by the realities of concrete, political issues. This discussion occupied even British publicists, and both sides had ample and contradictory material from Nietzsche's writings to support their positions.

The growth of Naziism shortly before and after Hitler's advent to power (1933) changed this picture. Hitler visited the Weimar Nietzsche archives several times, and Elisabeth, Nietzsche's sister, congratulated Mussolini on the occasion of his fiftieth birthday for being the "noblest disciple of Zarathustra." Nietzsche was made to serve the ideology of national-socialism, and an extensive popular literature grew quickly that added the philosopher to the long line of spiritual ancestors of the new political faith. Much of Nietzsche's contribution to the growth of national-socialism was made through the intellectual thievery and compulsory enlistment characteristic of Hitler's followers. Other phases of his writings seem to fall naturally into the Nazi pattern.

With Dostoevsky he shares the fate of having contributed to revolutionary mass movements of the greatest importance for history.

Nietzsche and Dostoevsky

> *Dostoevsky, the only one who has taught me anything about psychology.*
>
> *Nietzsche*

NIETZSCHE BECAME ACQUAINTED with some of Dostoevsky's works in 1887, after the death of the Russian; he speaks of Dostoevsky in connection with the Gospel's queer, sick world, of which the great Russian novelist had such rare understanding, and Dostoevsky seems to have influenced Nietzsche's image of Jesus, vacillating as it was between reverence and disdain.

At first, it must appear that Nietzsche and Dostoevsky lived poles apart. Dostoevsky's reverence for the anonymous little man, the humble saint and repentant sinner, stands in sharp contrast to Nietzsche's arrogant praise of the lonely superman and his haughty condescension toward the "much-too-many." Dostoevsky is apt to disappear behind his numerous characters or ever-changing plots, whereas Nietzsche never allows us to forget him on his solitary seat of judgment, from which he addresses mankind with vehement scorn.

Yet there were also surprising points of contact and even similarities.

Both belong to the order of the great confessors to whom mankind is indebted for some of its deepest insights into human nature. The title of Nietzsche's final self-description, *Ecce Homo,* was Pontius Pilate's last plea for mercy on behalf of Christ, a strange title to be chosen by the author of *The Antichrist*. Its self-revelation makes for painful and embarrassing reading. Even if we excuse his brazen self-glorification ("I will tell myself my own life") on the ground that it was written during his approaching insanity, the uncounted remarks about himself scattered over his entire work and correspondence are one huge monologue unveiling the innermost secrets of the lonely thinker. In a different manner but with the same counterpoint, the themes of Dostoevsky's novels are the reiterated variations of his own story: death sentences, commutation, deportation, epilepsy, gambling, religious doubt and self-torture, remorse, and the hate of Western civilization. His is a world of sickness; and Nietzsche could with reason regret that Dostoevsky had not been present in Jesus' own world, the illness and sin of which he would have interpreted with such understanding. Dostoevsky never realized his dream of writing several volumes on the project of atheism nor the autobiographical *Life of a Great Sinner,* but he endowed many of his characters with traits that were undoubtedly his own.

Both writers are passionately occupied with tearing from man the masks of pretension and morality. Nietzsche speaks of himself as dynamite; Dostoevsky's plots are nothing but the explosions of scandals and a succession of ridiculous, agonizing, and embarrassing scenes. Both feel that they are living outside the middle class to which they belong. Nietzsche was convinced that not Christian morality but the exalted spirit of life, the Greek *daimonion,* ought to motivate life. Dostoevsky saw this *daimonion* living in the unawakened collective genius of the Russian people, who would bring salvation to Europe and Asia, a faith Nietzsche shared at certain periods. The happiness of Russia would contain much suffering, as the genius of Nietzsche's superman was also burdened with sorrow. These predictions were, alas, fulfilled in our time in a most disturbing manner. Russian and German totalitarianism have indeed brought a full measure of sorrow and suffering.

For both the normal categories of well-being and health or illness are no longer sufficient to comprehend man's existence. Nietzsche considered a saint like Francis of Assisi a neurotic and epileptic visionary; Christianity was to him the result of hysteria and epilepsy. Dostoevsky's highest type, the idiot Prince Myshkin, suffers from epilepsy, the "sacred disease" that was also the writer's own tragic burden. Nietzsche proclaimed Christianity the religion of the herd-man, who is incapable of spirituality but only desires security, a thought expressed with equal cynicism by the Grand Inquisitor. But the Grand Inquisitor is yet superior to Nietzsche's superman. The cardinal feels at least some obligation to these "children," whereas Nietzsche holds them in disdain and would let them perish, maintaining that only the higher type of man is worthy of living.

Suffering occupies both thinkers, but they differ widely in its interpretation. Nietzsche would have agreed with Ivan Karamazov, who was willing to bring about mankind's happiness if it could be achieved by torturing to death one being, perhaps only a little child, whereas Alyosha, his brother, declared he would not be able to commit such cruelty under any circumstances.

Nietzsche's lifelong illness and his heroic resistance against it played such an important part in his creative thinking that he raised illness to the rank of a metaphysical order. Speaking of his personal experiences, he frequently tells how his own illness forced him to search for the meaning of life beyond that which is obvious, normal, and orderly. Illness and health are not contrasts but degrees of being. Illness raises creative man to that heroism which is the only condition from which great things arise. Illness produces, therefore, spiritual health. Overcoming illness generates ecstasy, whereas health tends to make man satisfied; it is a barrier keeping him from the ultimate recognition of life's secrets. Health can only serve to transcend illness.

Dostoevsky looks upon illness in a similar manner as a profound source of wisdom. His epilepsy subdues him with fatal regularity, but every one of his seizures is preceded by an overpowering and universal sense of harmony, producing a psychic happiness for which he was willing to give ten years of his life or even his entire life. Like Nietzsche, Dostoevsky realizes the enormous burden of illness and insanity laid upon those called to envision the ultimate truth. Both men are living in the vicinity of the abnormal and refuse to see an illness a weakness.

Just as they consider health and illness insufficient concepts, so do they regard the categories of moral good and evil as outworn and useless. Nietzsche's superman lives beyond good and evil. His question, "Nowadays, who knows still what is good and bad?" lights up with cynical candor the moral confusion and indifference that were beginning to be evident in Europe at the turn of the century. Dostoevsky states categorically, "There is no good and bad." His criticism resembles that of Nietzsche's "campaign against morality" in the *Dawn of the Day,* in which Nietzsche opposes normal ethical precepts and declares that the basis for all average virtue is sheer egoism, the desire to remain undisturbed and to be assured of salvation. Dostoevsky's Grand Inquisitor proclaims blatantly that only a few thousand can ever make the grade as true Christians, certainly not the millions who are calling themselves Christians.

In the vein of Kierkegaard's attacks, Nietzsche also maintains that "God is being strangled by theology," adding in like manner that "morals are choked off by the morality" of pretense and society's hypocrisy. The welter of chaos in Dostoevsky's creation is illustrated by the Grand Inquisitor, who contradicts Dostoevsky's own praise of the masses when he speaks of them as a harmonious ant heap, a trained horde of a hundred million. The cardinal and Kirillov in *The Possessed* are close relatives of Nietzsche, as are certain other characters in the Russian's stories.

Nietzsche and Dostoevsky wrestle with faith and doubt without ever being able to separate the two. Nietzsche's faith in the new man seems less tangible than his defiance of man as he saw him. His unceasing interior debate fuses doubt and belief into one as necessary concomitants. "I believe only by doubting whether I believe," he said. Dostoevsky's skepticism and outright admiration of doubt or unbelief reverse our concepts of sin and virtue in spite of the tenderness with which he surrounds his saints. It is more than a play on words when he says, "Man is a crook —and a crook is he who says so." Both fail in varying degrees to give a concrete goal to man.

Nietzsche's radical atheism finds, of course, no clearly approving balance in Dostoevsky's own wavering world of faith or disbelief, although we know how proud Dostoevsky was of the figure of Ivan Karamazov, who was a bolder embodiment of atheism than any earlier character. But Dostoevsky's Elder Zossima has a warm heart for atheists; he demands love for them because "there are many good ones among them." Even the criminals may be good men, the ones who had "the courage" to trespass and are now the "broken strong ones," a thought recurring with Nietzsche, who also believes in the essential psychological health of the criminal.

A love for the fatherland makes both Nietzsche and Dostoevsky elevate the soil to the same sacred category that has made the Russians the tenacious defenders of their country and that has given the Nazis their fanatical blood and soil gospel. Nietzsche's Zarathustra implores his audience to "remain true to our earth," while Dostoevsky's Zossima praises the sacredness of the soil and demands for it religious veneration.

The two writers belong to the great disturbers of humanity, and their uncanny premonition of the coming European disaster again links them together in many respects.

Their political visions deal with the future structure of all Europe or with limitless global schemes, just as their immediate counsel is at once specific and vague. Both share Kierkegaard's presentiment that Europe is doomed, and Nietzsche, who had never been in Russia, joins Dostoevsky in believing that Russia would yet have a mission of historic proportions.

A tragic but inevitable perversion of their ideas brought it about that both writers supplied energies of the most dynamic and destructive kind to later historic movements of which they could scarcely have approved. Dostoevsky's hope for Russia's future gave a voice to the latent messianic dreams in the modern Russian mind, without which contemporary bolshevism is unthinkable. Its inhuman and unchristian character would have aroused Dostoevsky's strongest protest, as may be seen in *The Possessed* and in the Grand Inquisitor's perverted gospel of the herd-man. It was symbolical that Dostoevsky prefaced this most revealing novel, which describes the world of cynical plotters and revolutionists, with the Gospel story of the Gadarene Swine (Mark V).

Wherever Dostoevsky expresses his hopes for the future power of Russia, there is an almost biblical atmosphere of expectancy, and his naïve faith in Christ's returning to Russia has now been turned into an anti-Christian political creed. Lenin has replaced this religious vision by "progress," and the organization of "happiness" by violence. It is, therefore, no accident that the Soviets tend to neglect Dostoevsky, the anti-socialist, considering him a bourgeois writer, and favor Leo Tolstoy, the epic chronicler of wars and the promoter of an ill-defined Christian socialism. Tolstoy's later non-violence and political anarchism would, undoubtedly, have turned him also against the present régime in Russia. But both Dostoevsky and Tolstoy have been feeding some of their energies into the bloodstream of Russian nationalism in a manner they could not possibly have foreseen.

Nietzsche likewise, by firing the imagination of German nationalism and strengthening the doctrine of racial superiority, has contributed to the catastrophic results of recent history. This must be said in spite of the fact that Hitler's vulgar figure was no incarnation of Nietzsche's superman and Naziism has drawn upon numerous other sources much more crucial and determining in their effects on politics than Nietzsche's philosophy. Among Nietzsche's own spiritual ancestors were men as diverse as Heinrich Heine, who wanted "hellenism" to combat "Nazarenism," and Ibsen with his vision of the Third Empire, a spiritual realm without plebeians, somewhat akin to the Third Rome of Dostoevsky's feverish fantasies. But many of Nietzsche's ideas became allies "in the spiritual warfare" of the Nazis, as one of their publicists wrote. Like Hitler, Nietzsche had been one of the "terrible simplifiers of history"—a term coined by Jakob Burckhardt, Swiss historian and friend of Nietzsche—and Naziism used him to seduce untold minds. His attacks upon the middle class, his "transvaluation of all values," his hostility to Christian morals, and his references to the "magnificent blond brute" and the "blond Teuton beast" (*Dawn of the Idols*) were gladly exploited by Hitler's disciples.

Nietzsche had felt repelled by anti-Semitism. As a writer he considered himself with the Jew Heinrich Heine the greatest figure in German literature. He had praised repeatedly the mental alertness of the Jewish race, and Wagner's anti-Semitism had been one of the reasons for the estrangement between the two geniuses. He was certainly not one to favor racial breeding for raising mankind's level. Nietzsche held other races in high regard, calling even Bismarck a Slav. In fact, he thought of the Germans as the "most mixed of all peoples" and denounced nationalism and race hatred (*The Gay Science*), stressing the need for being a good European. Yet the contradictory nature of much of his writing delivered convenient arguments into the hands of the Nazis, and history's judgment about his share of guilt in the perversion of the German mind will be less discerning than the thinker's own esoteric intentions might have wished.

Once more, it is a gross exaggeration to say that he is one of Naziism's immediate progenitors. Thomas Mann maintains rightly that it is more correct to say that fascism created Nietzsche than to contend that he created fascism. The ideas to which he gave his shrill articulation were a sensitive premonition of thoughts and moods vibrating in the minds of many Europeans. Dostoevsky in a similar manner divined those imperialistic trends in the Russian mind that have now dropped all pretense of the religious messianism in which he believed. Both men belong to the large group of thinkers, poets, historians, and prophets whose ideas have been made to serve as superstructure in the naked fight for power that no longer cares to disguise itself merely as a war of ideas.

Nietzsche's role in the thinking of mankind is certainly

not exhausted by such considerations. He is more than political dynamite. His thoughts were and will continue to be
the spiritual nutriment for many in this "age of longing"
(Koestler) who have lost their faith in religion, church,
politics, and society. This may seem strange in view of his
nihilism and chaos-creating denial of many of our traditional values. But Europe's mood must not be measured by
American standards, and Nietzsche's constructive influence
upon the religious thinking of European theology cannot at
this moment be fully appraised. The philosopher Karl
Jaspers leaves the question open as to his—and also
Kierkegaard's—ultimate meaning in mankind's history.
Much of what we can see in Nietzsche now is conditioned
by the spiritual substance with which we approach him.
He appears as mysterious to us as he was to himself. But
we know already that we cannot afford to ignore or
ridicule him.

Franz Kafka

> *The Messiah will come only when he is no longer needed . . .*

Chapter 1

ONCE, WHEN VISITING his friend and later biographer Max Brod, Franz Kafka noticed that Brod's father was sleeping in the anteroom where he had entered. Regretting that he had disturbed the old gentleman, he tiptoed out and whispered, "Please, consider me a dream." It was a considerate remark, and one that well characterizes Kafka's personality and his work.

Stig Dagerman, the Swedish Kafka of our time, once said of himself, "I don't dream when I sleep but when I am writing." Dagerman, trying to rise to a new "will to power" that would overcome fear, insecurity, and pessimism, also remarked, "We must remain loyal to our fears," and "We keep our fear open within us like a port free from ice where we can spend the winter."

Have these writers withdrawn from life and taken refuge in the uncharted regions of dreams and nightmares? Have they fallen in love with fear? Has life become unbearable for some among us who are too sensitive and sympathetic to the sufferings of our fellow men? Can we ever be too sensitive to the sufferings of others?

Chapter 2

IN CERTAIN PARTS of Burma it is customary for the friends of a dying man to assemble at his deathbed and remind him of the many good deeds he has done. This sacramental act of charity prepares him for the final step through the unknown gate, beyond which he then may confidently expect salvation, happiness, and eternal reward.

It is symptomatic that many of Europe's and America's writers who appeal to the conscientious reader consider our generation lost. Unlike the Burmese, their presence is accusing and their company conveys hardly a note of salvation or even the promise of healing. The shadows of despair and moral disintegration hover over vast numbers of their books. Nietzsche's prophecies about the post-Christian era that has already begun have provided disquieting illustrations in many of the supposedly noteworthy novels in this pitiless age.

Kafka's pageant of accusation occupies the foremost rank among the recent European prophecies of doom. A considerable time before the First World War and then in the years immediately following, he expressed the terror of life in such unforgettable images that comparisons with classical writers suggest themselves.

It has become customary to relate him to Kierkegaard, Dostoevsky, and Nietzsche—apart from others—but one wonders whether such honors are justified. He counted these three among the many spiritual forebears that served him in shaping his pessimistic dreams of man's destiny, but he had no share in passing on the greatness of their moral vision, their heroism in the face of defeat, or their transcendence beyond the human plane. He is, as it were, the outstanding heir of some of the debts to mankind which they left behind, their unpaid notes, their angry threats, and the uncanny rumors their voices had set in motion among the many who were unsure of the future. Kafka is the most existentialist among the existentialist writers employing insecurity and defeat as the fatalistic "solution" of that same sense of suspense and motion which Kierkegaard, Dostoevsky, and Nietzsche welcomed as the very element in which to rise above accident and fate. He expresses an existentialist *Weltgefühl* with stronger visionary force than his French colleagues, and speaks undoubtedly to the condition of untold men and women in Europe.

Chapter 3

AT ONE POINT the hero of Dostoevsky's *Letters from the Underground* declares solemnly that he had "often wished to become an insect" but never could achieve this weird ambition. Kafka's travelling salesman, Gregor Samsa, in the story *Metamorphosis* actually had this experience.

He awakens one morning to find himself changed into "some monstrous kind of vermin," a huge cockroach. He is still capable of thinking; his senses register the sounds and sight of his visiting family or acquaintances, but he is excluded from society. His mind is beyond communication. His own people leave him. There is no inward protest in Gregor Samsa; he only feels a "slight sorrow." For the rest, he accepts his fate with a matter-of-fact attitude.

Kafka's *The Penal Colony* conveys the same numb mood of resignation. The officer on duty describes details of a newly invented torturing machine to an "explorer" visiting the penal colony. The condemned men do not know their sentences; nor are they informed of the nature of their crimes. One of them will learn of his crime and the sentence when the command "Honor Your Superior" will be "inscribed" on his body by a harrow-like machine. Other prisoners may conclude from the length of their penalty how severe their crimes must have been.

The sad hero, Joseph K., not even bearing a full name, is accused in *The Trial* but does not know what constitutes his crime. The lawyers consider his situation difficult. Many other people seem to be informed about minute details of his case, but K. never learns the secret. He goes about his daily business as much as is still possible. Again during the actual trial held in a dark courtroom, he does not comprehend the charge against him, and when the sentence appears to have been passed upon him, he continues to be vague and even doubts later whether he is condemned. Two polite gentlemen visit him, take him away, and decapitate him. The moment before his death, K. only says, "Like a dog."

The visitor to the ruling aristocrat in *The Castle* never reaches the seat of the invisible potentate who had appointed him to serve as land surveyor. He remains in the village owned by the ruler; every attempt to see him is futile. There is no connection between the village and the castle. Without losing patience, the land surveyor tries again and again to reach the ruler. As with Camus' Sisyphus, every failure is succeeded by a new and futile effort. Over the telephone he hears a vague kind of laughter, and distant silence reigns at other moments. One of the women in the village remarks how sorry she feels about another attempt that will be probably futile. Another day will be "probably futile"; to continue hoping will be "probably vain." There is something ominous about these endless attempts that remind one of Nietzsche's dangerous "perhaps." K., who this time does not even bear a first name, tries to become one of the villagers himself and embarks upon some erotic adventures. He attaches himself finally to a family not subject to the ruler; again he remains excluded.

In *The Burrow* man changes into some kind of animal, building one protective outlet after another. *The Hunter Gracchus* has died long ago but cannot leave the world of the living. The captain of the boat that was to carry him to the land of the dead had made a mistake when steering the ship. The hunter is always on the "great stairway leading upward" but can neither leave nor arrive. Gracchus, like Samsa or K., cannot participate in life.

Chapter 4

THERE ARE SIMILARLY fantastic stories in which the dead rise, a mouse worries, a dog investigates life. In one, a bridge turns and looks around, and in others the laws of physics do not apply but seem suspended as they are in dreams. The setting of these stories remains curiously vague. While different each time, the normal order tends to give way to the grotesque, absurd, or perverted. Nature delivers hardly any of its paraphernalia to Kafka. Many of his tales do not mention flowers, trees, sunshine, or landscape. As in the work of Melville, Kafka's women are insignificant; his world is that of men. His people do not develop; they have no "will to power" and no personality. The atmosphere in which they live reminds one of Alfred Kubin's ghostly sketches, or Salvador Dali's synthetic dream portraits, and they convey the dread and fright that pervade many of Edvard Munch's paintings. These uncanny sensations seem to rise of their own volition in the reader, who will not find them suggested in Kafka's style.

Kafka writes a clear and pleasant German prose, and much of it is close to perfection in spite of his verboseness and the tendency of his characters to argumentative reflection. His style employs no staccato emphases; everything flows on in calm, epic sentences with scarcely a hint at coming catastrophe. The characters appear not at all terrorized, and their conversations frequently dwell on the little details of daily life. A sense of bureaucratic order surrounds the most dismal scenes, giving them a finality that renders them all the more eerie. Whatever Kafka's interpreters may read into his stories, it seems certain that he is a master of subtle understatement, an art so rarely practiced in German literature that the German language contains no term fully equivalent to the English word "understatement."

Much of Kafka's work was unfinished when he died. Perhaps it is this absence of solutions in his own life as well as in his work that makes these stories more symbolical than he may have intended—and also more prophetic than he could have known. He died in 1924, ten years before the world had ever heard about the concentration camps which were clairvoyantly forecast in *The Penal Colony* and in some scenes of *The Trial*, even to the minutiae of the later Nazi uniforms.

His world knows no physical or moral order; the paradox rules; the absurd or contradictory factors that had been a spiritually valid element in Kierkegaard's thinking, in Dostoevsky's sinners and saints, and in Nietzsche's superhuman attempt to transcend life, became the exclusive and negative order in Kafka's world. His characters know of no resurrection as do the best of Dostoevsky's men and women. The prevailing mood of fear is there, but the emotional reaction is lacking in the men and women on Kafka's stage. We, the readers, are reliving our bad dreams. The crime-and-punishment themes of Dostoevsky are inverted; punishment is over all the characters, but the crime remains mysteriously hidden.

Kafka's main theme, then, is an ever-present sense of guilt, perhaps sin, and this guilt is being revenged on those who are unable to recognize their moral burden. Otto Weininger, one of Kafka's Jewish contemporaries, makes it a point to assign to memory a predominantly moral function. It is much more than the archive of intellectual or sense impressions; it registers good and evil with omniscient accuracy, and God's terrible threat to punish sin and guilt even to the third and fourth generation may have inspired Weininger and Kafka alike. The fact that some of Kafka's characters do not know of their guilt receives an added interest from the psychoanalytical experience that the true object of any analysis is not the recovery of earlier and disturbing traumas but the recall of the lost memory of them. The crux of the problem is this passive transcendence of the mind into a seemingly unrecoverable past: we have forgotten that we have forgotten.

This double absence of memory reminds one of Kierkegaard's remark that he "who lives ethically has memory of his life, whereas he who lives aesthetically has not." Only those who are striving for moral perfection are, therefore, "existing."

The guilty ones in Kafka's stories are surrounded by others who seem neutral, although not always indifferent; but they never reduce the sense of solitude in the guilty ones. There is none of Dostoevsky's all-guilt, the fraternal oneness sensation, or a vicarious suffering that has a redemptive quality. All is numbness, and the surprises of grace of which Charles Péguy speaks and which Kierkegaard and Dostoevsky know so abundantly, are absent.

God has indeed died.

Chapter 5

DOSTOEVSKY'S PROPHECY that anything will be permitted if man gives up believing in God, Nietzsche's "universal madness," predicted for the coming age of atheism, these apply to the world of soundless and swift disaster of Kafka, who was neither an atheist nor one capable of rallying himself to a strong affirmation of his Jewish faith. Kafka's men are living in that world without God of which Nietzsche predicted that it would be somehow older, strange, and suspicious, a late hour of mankind.

Apart from minor characters, Kafka's marionettes are either victims or executioners. Totalitarianism as it swept over Central Europe ten years after Kafka's death, treated Jews and political nonconformists like vermin, to be annihilated or abandoned like Gregor Samsa in *Metamorphosis*. It is interesting to remember in this connection that Dostoevsky's superman, Raskolnikov, before murdering the pawnbroker, heard his friends speaking of her as "a louse, a black beetle," a remark that influenced him to think of his crime as "an experiment," a term not unknown to the Nazi vocabulary of concentration camp "medicine." Totalitarianism held mock trials such as Joseph K. had in *The Trial*. As in *The Castle*, there was no recourse to the remote lord of justice for whom Kafka longed, but only distant silence or vague laughter. The dead have not been laid to rest: the conscience of generations will be pained by their return to conscious memory, as the hunter Gracchus, innocent of any guilt of his own, continues to visit the living.

Günther Anders, one of Kafka's German interpreters, likens Kafka's technique to that of Aesop, whose fables were meant to convey the lesson that men are like animals; therefore Aesop makes animals act like men. Kafka, in a similar inversion of reality, makes the terrible seem natural because he considers the natural terrible. The sense of suspense in Kierkegaard, Dostoevsky, and Nietzsche has now become a motion downward no longer to be arrested. The world is a dark beyond, an uncontrollable autonomy of horror without moral rules or recognizable significance. Our moral code no longer suffices to master it, and there is no way out. And since we do not know its laws, we all are guilty.

It would, however, be unfair to ascribe to Kafka the conscious proclamation of contempt for morality or theism. If one wants to find a message in his work, then his little fable of the "couriers," a piece of less than a hundred words, conveys it effectively. The people had the choice of becoming kings or the kings' couriers. After the manner of children—the Grand Inquisitor speaks of men as irresponsible children—they all wanted to be couriers (who had no vision of a king's responsibilities and no desire to assume moral leadership). Now the world is full of couriers who are shouting senseless messages at each other. They realize this state of affairs but refrain from committing suicide(!) because of their oath of service and loyalty; the "much-too-many" continue to live morally because of fear and obedience, not from inner freedom. Their message is without meaning (or moral strength), and all is anxiety and despair.

A good deal of theorizing about Kafka's philosophy has searched for the theological camouflage that his work is supposed to represent. Guilt, punishment, and the unbridgeable chasm between the lord in *The Castle* and the despairing visitor suggest some relationship to Barth's unfathomable otherness and remoteness of God. Kafka's Jewishness has been quoted as the basic motive for his radical denial of resurrection and salvation. The Jewish God—so argues, for example, the Catholic Ignaz Zangerle—is not the ever-present God of Christianity but has disappeared behind his laws. He is at best an idea, a burning bush, a faint memory, but not a person.

The impressive absence of hope in Kafka's work gives it the most telling note if one looks for religious symbolism. All of Kafka's characters have lost the paradise of God's nearness. Eternity has been replaced by endlessness. Kierkegaard's paradox of God's love for man, this center of all faith, absurd and unbelievable to our human logic, this love is alien to Kafka's thinking. Absent, therefore, is the mysterious act of forgiveness which is one of Kierkegaard's axioms and Dostoevsky's ever-repeated resurrection miracle. Job's loneliness and despair reign, but God is missing. Kafka's stories represent the extreme polarity of Voragine's *Legenda Aurea,* the golden book of legends of medieval saints. They are the *Legenda Nigra;* his characters are made to live the *via negativa,* and one may well call his fascinating and disquieting work the anti-gospel of Nietzsche's post-Christian era.

Chapter 6

CHARLES BAUDELAIRE IN FRANCE (1821–1867) inaugurated that phase in European literature which gravitates around man's loneliness and isolation and has prepared us for the contemporary literature of extreme situations. The poet-thinker, Baudelaire, removed himself from his fellow man in the schizoid sensation of superiority and unworthiness. He accused himself less than life's darkness and confusion. The depressing experiences of the last thirty years have swept away the last remnants of the belief that man's destiny shares in the guided continuity of history, and it is more than a literary fashion that such half-forgotten poets and writers as Arthur Rimbaud, Léon Bloy, and Ernest Hello are now having their renaissance in France. All of them had expressed social alienation, and in their hostility to recognized middle-class standards they attacked Church and religion as part of society's interior milieu.

The contemporary school of pseudo-existentialistic *belles lettres* extols this aloneness in life and dwells on its senseless character. We cannot help going on living. There is this inescapable fact of existing in suspense, and absurdly enough, we are "free" in our decisions (Sartre), but there is no longer an essence or existence that gives meaning to this freedom. Moral action becomes, therefore, anachronistic. Man is, at long last, beyond good and evil. He has lost all inward ties to his fellow man because he recognizes no deity. Ever-present fear is now his lot. He must choose without knowing which choice to make. The superhistorical heritage of Moses' decalogue or the Sermon on the Mount are considered no longer applicable to the chaos of our age. W. H. Auden's verdict is to the point when he says, "Existentialism has, as Baudelaire said of stoicism, one sacrament for the sinner—suicide." Both Sartre and Camus are, however, aware that Baudelaire's detachment from society was nothing but another *Trahison des Clercs,* and they want to take an active share in politics. They oppose Stalinism, capitalism, and Christianity without being able to make a choice or offer a new political creed.

Léon Bloy and George Bernanos impress us as fearless critics of the Catholic Church, of which nevertheless they remained loyal members. Their skill in portraying infernal characters, some of them Catholic priests, as we find them also in Graham Greene's works, and the apparent delight with which they reflect the ever-present power of moral and social evil cannot, however, make them spiritual relatives of Sartre and Camus. Theologically speaking, they are dramatizing their conviction that the devil's power has enormously increased in our time; but, as in Job, the devil is still God's servant, not His adversary. Their faith in God leads them to a new search for His will in the jungles of modern city life, and their dark narratives have some of the force of Holbein's religious cartoons and Stephan Lochner's hell scenes, where we see sinful popes suffering with other condemned souls.

Their new religious expression revives the apocalyptic fears of former centuries. George Bernanos writes that evil in our time is only in its first beginning, a message echoed by Nicholas Berdyaev's emphasis that the future power of evil will be more terrible than at any earlier time. In contrast to these, C. S. Lewis' *Screwtape Letters,* with their concessions to modern man's desire for entertainment, make pleasant reading for the timid skeptics. It is as though the thin distribution of morality in Christian society is expected to find in such artistic renditions of novelists and painters a catalyst to produce the first crystallization of a new faith. The modern Christian writer with artistic leanings wants to wean man away from the aesthetic to the moral by giving his art a moral cast.

Kafka had no such aims. He centered upon darkness. In

a sense he had the evil eye capable of the most luminous penetration of this darkness. He was a disturber, and Günther Anders—to return to his theological interpreters—considers it his salvation that he was hopelessly skeptical toward his own work. We know how he suffered from his sympathies with human beings and animals. He, the Jew by background and longing although not by conviction, brings it home to us that the so-called Jewish question is eminently a Christian problem.

Chapter 7

THE LIFE OF Franz Kafka was rather uneventful. Born in 1883 in Prague, Bohemia, then part of the Austrian empire, the son of a prosperous merchant, he took his law degree in 1906. Two years later he accepted a position in the government-sponsored Workers' Accident Insurance. In 1909 he published his first small pieces in literary periodicals and newspapers, his "one desire and calling" being literature. His modest and rather sporadic successes as a writer forced him to remain in his original position until he was retired because of his tuberculosis, from which he died at forty-one, in 1924.

His father had no understanding of Franz's literary interests, and the unhappy relationship between the two was one of unrelieved tension. Franz Kafka dissolved his engagement to Miss F. B.; a second friendship again did not lead to marriage. As in the case of Kierkegaard, this unhappy relationship with father and fiancée have given rise to many psychological interpretations of the Freudian school. Kafka's friendship with Max Brod, his later biographer, and other artists in prewar Prague enriched his otherwise melancholy and frustrated life. Brod did not execute Kafka's last will to destroy the manuscripts but saved them for posterity. Their friendship dated back to 1902, when Brod discovered Kafka's literary gifts and persuaded him to publish his first pieces.

The Prague of 1910–1914, where Kafka had his first small successes, produced and attracted diverse talents. Here Franz Werfel wrote his early stories and small plays. Hugo v. Hofmansthal, Rilke, and others met in the twilight atmosphere of these years with Kafka, Brod, and their friends in literary cafés. The wealth of stimulation seemed to create a paradise for which Smetana's music furnished the sensual comfort. Nijinsky danced at the opera. The little group of literateurs, mostly Jewish, wrote, translated, and debated the future; one of them speaks later about Kafka's silent presence, his elusive smiles, and perennial melancholy. Some made a trip to Dresden, where G. B. Shaw was, Paul Claudel, and some members of the Russian nobility; here they attended rare theatrical events. They read Kierkegaard, Dostoevsky, Tolstoy, and Pascal, but apart from the unhappy official in the Workers' Insurance, they lived in aesthetic detachment from the stream of life to which millions of their Czech compatriots belonged. They felt at home in the realm of the arts for arts' sake and did not, or perhaps could not, realize that Kierkegaard's condemnation of the aesthetic life would actually become part of the despair and tragedy into which ancient Prague, and especially its Jewish population, was to be later immersed.

As Kafka's *Diary* indicates, he was aware of the lack of any true foundation for life, of air, and of a guiding code and commandment. It was his fate not to be able to seize the "last tip" of the Jewish prayer shawl. As a youth he had felt critical about Jewish rituals and beliefs, and his later interest in Judaism, including Zionism, remained fairly mild. He refers in like manner to his inability to be guided, "like Kierkegaard," by the "sinking hand" of Christianity.

History dealt harshly with Prague. Perhaps it was only Kafka who had foreseen in his oppressive dreams what was to happen. The ordinary people, the petty officials and strangers in the street who fill Kafka's stage with their mute presence, rose to hate and crime in the Nazi movement. The masses everywhere dressed up in fantastic uniforms such as they had worn in some of Kafka's tales thirty years earlier and burned down synagogues, forcing yellow marks of ostracism or the Star of David on Jewish homes, clothes, and stores, while the voices of invisible speakers aroused these minor characters to monstrous, incredible deeds. No Christian group in modern history has suffered as much as the Jews under Hitler, and Kierkegaard's words, "To live as Christians in this world means to suffer," may give us pause when we compare the martyrdom of the Jews with the cruelty of their "Christian" persecutors.

These persecutions claimed victims from Kafka's own family. Three of his sisters and several other relatives died in the Auschwitz extermination camp. And one of the few houses destroyed during the 1945 liberation of Prague was Kafka's parental home.

Chapter 8

ALTHOUGH KAFKA'S DIARIES are full of bizarre day and night dreams, his warm human heart made it impossible for him to overlook the realities of life. His position at the Workers' Accident Insurance afforded many contacts with those whose claims came to his desk, and he once remarked in a mixture of admiration and impatience how humble these little people were. Their situation occupied him to such an extent that he even projected a scheme for improving society, a plan which he dropped later in his creative period. But he shared Henry David Thoreau's conclusion that "the mass of men lead lives of quiet desperation."

It is interesting that Kafka was one of the first to touch upon the despair of a key figure in the economic system that is now engaged in a life and death struggle in Europe, the salesman whose function in free enterprise is that of a missionary. Gregor Samsa in Kafka's *Metamorphosis* suffers from the same overpowering sense of futility as his French colleague of a generation later, Monsieur Martin, in Jean Anouilh's *Pièces Noires*. Both of them escape into dream life or insanity, and both their stories suggest more clearly the breakdown of society than Arthur Miller's *Death of a Salesman*, in which Willy Loman's fate remains a personal tragedy within an otherwise normal, or at least self-assured, society.

Kafka was hardly a reformer. He was, likewise, not a great thinker, philosopher, or theologian. There remains something enigmatic about him that eludes classification. His own life was not the exclusive key to an understanding of his work; yet it speaks to the condition of many who are searching for the causes of our present moral exhaustion. His life may be, after all, symbolical of some of

Europe's problems. It was perhaps less important that he was alienated from society, his family, and his profession. These were a tragic condition all the harder to endure as society denied him the recognition as a writer which he is now receiving posthumously. But that his clairvoyant vision failed to transcend life's obstacles and experience man's victories of faith, or even man's capacity for endurance, that was his real tragedy. He could not envision the meaning of suffering.

He is passing on this problem to us in the imperishable images of his art. Is this Kafka's way of indirect communication? Is it a reproach to the Christian believer whose Church knows so much about the meaning of suffering while its members have done so little to prevent it?

Is Kafka's mute query rising from his grave now as some of his characters used to return to the living, unable to find their rest?

The Four Apocalyptic Horsemen

> *And the angel thrust his sickle into the earth, and gathered the vine of the earth, and cast it into the great winepress of the wrath of God.*
>
> *Revelation, XIV:19*

THESE FOUR WRITERS, Kierkegaard, Dostoevsky, Nietzsche, and Kafka, occupy, each in his own peculiar way, the position of outsiders in the society that had produced them. They lived the insecure existence of spiritual frontiersmen who no longer fit into the accepted categories of theology, philosophy, or *belles-lettres,* and can see during their lifetime no immediate chance for getting the hearing they deserve. They realized that they were both the end products of a dying civilization and the clairvoyant prophets of coming chaos. Kierkegaard's judgment of himself as an "enigma," and Kafka's self-characterization as "an end or a beginning" pertain to all four.

Their contemporaries dismissed their dark premonitions as exaggerated, unbelievable, or outright fantastic. European society took one of three positions: it was satisfied with its own apparent stability, or believed in the general progress of mankind, or favored some mild reforms while the political revolutionists were demanding the radical overthrow of the entire existing social organism. Kafka was resigned to the coming triumph of evil, which the other three had also considered a powerful threat or the alarm signal for rallying counter-energies. But Kierkegaard, Dostoevsky, and Nietzsche expected a new phase in mankind's history to rise that would fulfill their spiritual visions, a kingdom to follow disasters of apocalyptic dimensions. Their emphasis on evil marks them as eschatological writers.

Apart from the recognition that came to Dostoevsky in his later years, the world did not accept the messages of these writers during their lifetimes. Kierkegaard had to wait half a century or more; Nietzsche's importance increased with each decade after his death; and Kafka's larger novels were not published until after he had died. He is now slowly emerging from the rank of a bizarre outsider whose work is still considered experimental.

All four have a greater capacity for defining critical aspects of humanity's condition than for giving voice to concrete leadership or to a specific vision of humanity's future. With the exception of Kierkegaard, whose firmly maintained Lutheran theology was his salvation, they seemed at times to surrender to the *via negativa* of personal weakness, anxiety, and physical illness, but apart from Kafka they rose again and again to heroic visions. Dostoevsky and Nietzsche cherished the deviation from the normal as a stimulant, ordained by fate to strengthen the will to resist, to live more exaltedly, and to probe more deeply into the mysteries of existence.

Not only do these four stand outside the accepted categories of literature by uniting the functions of psychologist, philosopher, poet, sociologist, and critic in their diagnoses of Europe's spiritual disintegration, but through their work they were also instrumental in speeding up the actual process of the destruction they foresaw. Their voices stirred up such intensely partisan response that only our generation is beginning to see in them more than destructive forces. Their marginal position in society, productive but unintegrated, appealed to many in their own social group who likewise remained unabsorbed, had become resentful, and consequently felt inspired by the contempt these writers were expressing for the middle class.

Much of their fate as human beings lends itself to interesting comparisons and even a few striking parallels. Their spiritual biographies are partially explained by the circumstances in which they grew, lived, and worked. But in no case do these conditions supply us with the complete means for interpreting their spiritual course.

All four were suspicious of man's pretenses before himself and others. They vehemently accused their contemporaries, especially those of the middle class, with not living up to any, or very few, of their publicly proclaimed moral standards. Kierkegaard calls the Church a sham that is making "a fool of God." Dostoevsky never tires of revealing the many demons lurking in every human being beneath a respectable surface and even within the Church itself. For Nietzsche both Christianity and the middle class are stupid, anachronistic, and suspect. Kafka knows of no brave men to oppose the forces of a conniving and scheming evil at work everywhere. Society, to him, is unprincipled. It was his conviction that the hand of Christianity was weakening.

All four were alien to the society in which they lived, and their contempt for respectability was deeply rooted in childhood experiences. A sense of aloneness and disillusionment overshadowed their early years, in which a father's strength and affection were missing and in which neither admiration nor the early assurance of parental protection could develop. Kierkegaard's father was a man of religious gloom; the discovery of his erotic defections made such a shocking impression upon Sören that he speaks of it as "an earthquake." Dostoevsky's father was callous and intemperate, in many ways resembling the ill-fated elder Karamazov, and was, like him, murdered when Dostoevsky was still an adolescent. Nietzsche's father died when Friedrich was only four years old. Kafka's father, a successful but sarcastic business man, remained without understanding for his son's genius. Only such tragic conditions could produce Ivan Karamazov's perverted excuse at the murder trial when he said, "Who does not desire his father's death?" and Nietzsche's pathetic outcry, "What child has not had reason to weep over his parents?"

Their relationship to their fatherland is as ambivalent as their negative position in society. Kierkegaard seems to have only critical things to say about Denmark. Many of his intellectual roots were in the Germany of Hegel and Schelling, while his criticism of the Danish Church developed rapidly into isolation and finally open hostility. The satirical attacks of *The Corsair* drove him close to despair;

he felt ostracized and solitary, the butt of public ridicule.

Dostoevsky's love for Russia was, apart from his final panslavic phase, an unhappy one, while his inner relationship to Western Europe vacillated between admiration and hate. He was unhappy in Russia but could not have borne the emigrant's lot of not living on her soil. After the sudden fame of his *Poor People,* he remained unsuccessful for a considerable period, never overcoming the resentment against a society that had considered him socially awkward and uncouth. It was only one of the many contradictions in his psyche that he did not attack Russia politically for the wrongs suffered during his Siberian exile.

Nietzsche lived outside Germany from his twenty-fifth year on and became one of his fatherland's most embittered critics, projecting himself in his imagination as one living the life of a Greek god or prophet in Olympian ecstasy, never at home in the world of reality, yet at the same time harboring typically German romantic dreams of the kind that have contributed to the malignant growth of intellectual Naziism.

Kafka, the Jew, was removed from the world of Judaism and critical of Christianity. As a German-speaking Czech, he was not quite a German; nor was he a *Volksdeutscher.* Working as he did in the social security board that served primarily the laboring class, he did not belong to this social group; nor did he quite belong to the middle class. He was an ordinary official, a functionary; yet writing was his real calling. His work in an insurance concern reflects ironically upon his own perennial social and spiritual insecurity.

All four had prepared themselves during their early manhood for a profession recognized by their own class as respectable and orderly, but all four failed to pursue their original profession in their mature years. Kierkegaard, trained for pastoral duties, refused to accept a pastorate and considered writing his ordained vocation, a vocation in which he excelled as a humorist, satirist, polemicist, and exegetic scholar as well as a philosopher. His rare achievement is all the more remarkable in view of his torrential production within a brief compass of time. Dostoevsky abandoned his military career for the uncertainties of journalism and free-lance writing. Nietzsche was a classical scholar of the rarest promise, feeling completely at home in Greek antiquity. He turned to reforming mankind and produced a philosophy in which poetry, prophecy, and fantasy are fused in a hitherto unknown amalgamation and clothed in such a brilliant style that he ranks among the classic writers of the German language. Kafka, the jurist and official, tried himself out as a free-lance writer but was forced to consider himself a failure to his dying day.

They were lonely men and suffered intensely from the feeling of having remained unloved. They had, therefore, the urge to reveal themselves to their contemporaries or to posterity, and all four had that passion for confession of which Otto Weininger said, "Great men speak and write only about themselves." Kierkegaard's entire work, especially his diary, lays bare his spiritual pains apart from the explicit references to his unhappy love for Regine Olsen. Dostoevsky never executed his original plan to write the confessional novel, *The Life of a Great Sinner,* but many of his characters undoubtedly reflect his own inner conflicts. Nietzsche, "self-knower and self-executioner," presents in his letters rich autobiographical material, with strangely metaphysical analyses of his illness, and before the outbreak of his insanity, with detailed psychological self-portraits. Kafka's *Diary* is full of reflections about himself, as are his letters.

All four were physically weak or sick. Three of them, Kierkegaard, Nietzsche, and Kafka, ended their literary production in their forties. Kierkegaard died at forty-two, Kafka at forty-one. Nietzsche was a sick man during his entire adult life. Dostoevsky suffered most of his life from epileptic seizures. With the exception of Kafka, they showed great heroism in the face of physical adversity, and their attitude is the perfect fulfillment of Pascal's "Prayer to God for the Right Use of Illness." The thinking of all four occupied itself with suffering. Kierkegaard regarded it as the beginning of all spiritual insight; Dostoevsky saw in it the key to understanding others; Nietzsche felt it was an obstacle to be overcome. Only Kafka let it be a cruel and senseless fact.

In their relationship to women all four were unhappy. Kierkegaard and Kafka broke their engagements, and, like Nietzsche, never married. Nietzsche probably never had a genuine love experience. Dostoevsky's love life was a succession of unhappy adventures until he was past middle age and entered a marriage of convenience; none of his novels depicts a happy marriage.

None of the four believed firmly in his success as a thinker or writer. Moments of arrogance or justified pride alternated with long-lasting depressions. With the exception of Kafka, all considered passion, enthusiasm, and the intoxicating sense of mission and inspiration their realm. In this they were truly displaced persons in the original meaning of the word (*ekstasis*), and Kierkegaard as well as Nietzsche employed the imagery of the dance to express this mood. After some initial successes both Kierkegaard and Nietzsche had to finance their own publications. The dying Kafka, little known as a writer, implored his friend Max Brod to burn all his unprinted works, after having himself destroyed, in all likelihood, some manuscripts at an earlier time. Dostoevsky was successful after a severe struggle but hardly ever found the time to polish his works. As with Balzac, his perennial indebtedness to publishers forced him to hasty production, although his final years gave him a period of quiet and recognition.

All four were city men who sensed that the cities would witness first the oncoming degradation of society. But none applied the amply available arguments of science or sociology to the prognosis of Europe's downfall. Each visualized it as the inevitable result of a spiritual crisis, different as the diagnosis of this crisis was in the mind of each.

There is a continuity of purpose and motivation in the work of these four that is more significant than literary influences can be. But Dostoevsky and Kierkegaard did not know of each other. Nietzsche never read a single line of Kierkegaard's writings, and did not carry out his intention of studying the "psychological problem of Kierkegaard" but he did know some of Dostoevsky's chief novels. From the first reading he sensed an instinctive and strange affinity with the Russian and felt "intoxicated" by Dostoevsky's bold psychological penetration of man's innermost impulses. But Nietzsche could never go beyond admiring Dostoevsky as a unique psychologist and remained alien to the Christian note in his works. Both drew many of their prophetic energies from dreamlike moods, emotional states of exaltation, and visions of indefinable scope.

In their universalism and breadth of vision, at least Nietzsche and Dostoevsky have something of the *uomo universale* of the Renaissance, which Dostoevsky expressed in his hope that his projected *Life of a Great Sinner* would bring forth a concrete vision of "world harmony," a goal alien to the austere demands of Kierkegaard and the moral exhaustion of Kafka.

The Angel's Finger

> *And the winepress was trodden without the city, and blood came out of the winepress, even unto the horse's bridles, by the space of a thousand and six hundred furlongs.*
>
> *Revelation XIV:20*

In Dürer's Woodcut "The Four Apocalyptic Horsemen" (1498), the four horsemen are not permitted to drop their dark messages where they please; they are being directed by God's angel whose finger guides them. Evil and catastrophe are clearly understood to be part of a design that will ultimately reveal God's plan, hidden at present to the human mind.

Such a theological interpretation, though not pleasing to much of our contemporary western thinking, yet leaves a broad margin for human self-examination, a critical surveying of our own doings such as contemporary Europe is undertaking now with more candor and humility than some of our political observers seem to realize; some still erroneously report that there is no change of mind in the European psyche. There can be no doubt that a religious rebirth of profound seriousness is developing within Protestantism, Catholicism, and among the refugee Orthodox groups of Western Europe. Kierkegaard, Dostoevsky, and Nietzsche are among the guiding spirits from whose spiritual resources this Christian renaissance is drawing much energy. Literary existentialism of the atheistic school supplies additional, though negative, substantiation of these new insights, if only through its contrasting visions of despair.

Kierkegaard stands out as the one whose incisive truths and courageous personal fight have inspired the modern mind to move beyond the province of neo-orthodox thinking. He has opened our eyes to the shallowness of much of our pseudo-Christian life and to the outright deception in politics which Christianity has been made to serve. Europe is beginning to recognize the spiritual origin of the recent catastrophes.

Kierkegaard had excommunicated himself from a sense of scrupulous sincerity, while many in official Christianity were silently slipping away from the inward ties to faith, and had been, figuratively speaking, excommunicated from the "Invisible Church" before they realized it. God had become as much a matter of the past, a remote memory, as materialistic society is in danger of making Him. Then as now, membership in the Christian church was indeed part of a family inheritance, an heirloom of antiquarian value, whereas Kierkegaard demanded that we "recollect forward" in an effort at *becoming,* not *being,* Christians. The moral core of Kierkegaard's attack upon the unholy marriage of state and church is widely accepted by Europe's present generation, but its spiritual implications are only beginning to be understood, and no drastic changes have yet been made in the relationship of state and church.

Kierkegaard's emphasis upon Christianity's prophetic mission is also receiving more of a hearing by Church leaders and laymen than during his own time. The Universal Church is beginning to realize that it must not confine itself to representing the moral factor in the Christian message. It can never be an assembly of the righteous but must go out to find those who are in need of its healing and prophetic message.

We are learning that contradiction and condemnation are not creative. The judgment theology of Barth and Brunner has contributed a note of self-examination to our thinking. We are too apt to identify the gospel message with man's endeavor to create God's Kingdom. The rejection of a "service-minded" liberalism is, on the other hand, too convenient a way out of our dilemma, just as the theologians' flight from the immediate political and social urgencies of our time into an artificial and antiquarian orthodoxy is unacceptable to many conscientious seekers who look upon this orthodoxy as a serious loss of Christian energies.

Not only the Church, or Christianity, or our so-called Christian society are in need of salvation. Vast segments of this society which are pagan, alien, or hostile to faith are in need of the Christian ministry. All too often this ministry is obscured by professional language understandable only to the trained mind. And all too often ritual and liturgical adornment becomes the easy way out for official Christianity as it seeks to deepen spiritual life. Kierkegaard's rejection of the aesthetic way of life opens an attack upon this sentimental Sunday Christianity, with the atmosphere of respectable society, polished oratory, and decorative representation.

The example of a few Catholic and Protestant clerics and laymen in the mining districts of Belguim, France, and Germany, where these men and women work day after day in factory and mine with proletarians who have never heard of the Christian message, testifies to a new heroism and realism of faith. This faith is as far removed from the controversies of theological seminars as from a shallow middle-class liberalism that has frequently considered its suburban comfort a God-given reward for sound moral standards. Kierkegaard invites all of us to become first and foremost citizens in the Kingdom of Anxiety. He demands a way of life, an existential faith. The self-assurance of belief is as objectionable as that of disbelief, while the indifference of the lukewarm is nothing but self-deception or an outright betrayal of the Christian cause.

In like manner does Dostoevsky's chaotic world attack much of our Christian society, where everything seemed well-ordered in the hierarchy of society and in the moral representation of faith by the clergy. Some of his magnificent sinners find their way to God through other sinners, some few through the wisdom of official spiritual leaders. His great merit lies in dramatizing man's dualism. We live in the world of conscious error or virtue, but we are also prey to the subconscious forces, the illogical drives, that cause the unexpected eruptions of instincts and resentments, the hidden motives for hypocrisy and the condemnation of others that shake individuals and society out of their sense of security.

The hoped-for security should be understood primarily as a spiritual state, a *charisma* that puts the burden of ministry on everyone who is thus graced. Dostoevsky himself never experienced this state with any permanence, and those few of his characters who have it see an endless stream of sinners and confused seekers coming to them for spiritual assistance. It is not their theology but their existence as humble Christians that attracts those in despair. Dostoevsky makes his point in contrasting extremes; the invisible Church loves, forgives, and understands, whereas the Grand Inquisitor, the outstanding representative of the visible Church, condemns others, although he himself is in great need of forgiveness. The works of mercy are hidden, for God's own hand works in secret.

The legend of the Grand Inquisitor is an attack upon all churchdom and all human prominence in the household of God. Its paradoxical proclamation that man does not want to be free is better understood in the second half of the twentieth century than in 1880. It was a shock to the European and American mind to see how seemingly progressive nations acted precisely as the Grand Inquisitor had prophesied by laying down their freedom at the feet of rulers in exchange for bread and security. Many of our humanistic dreams for mankind have proved illusory, and because of these disillusioning experiences all of us are now displaced people, in some sense *déracinés*. Our moral and political freedom is now being recognized as the great burden which the Grand Inquisitor made it in his prison monologue. The fact that large nations (Germany, Japan, Russia, China) are either not ready for freedom or reject it as impracticable stands in such appalling contrast to our American tradition that many of us have found it easier to attribute this state of affairs to the conspiracy of a few leaders abroad. We shall have to acquire a considerably greater sense of perspective and a sounder knowledge of the history, language, and literature of these nations to come closer to the truth.

As we have tried to illustrate, much of Dostoevsky's prophecy—too much for our comfort—has proved to be true. His claims for the Russian people as a "God-bearing" nation, capable as no other nation of understanding all the world, though part of the neurotic universalism that characterized him personally as well as many other Russian leaders, have contributed to the dynamism of the bolshevistic revolution. This belief exists and always has existed in Russia, where the ikons of Lenin and Stalin inspire it daily. National self-exaltation also exists in non-communist nations, where not only political leaders but also poets and historians have been spreading an incendiary patriotism of self-righteousness that has caused their peoples to look down upon other nations and to become outright threats to peace.

Moscow, we now know, will not be the Third Rome of which the panslavists were dreaming. But it is our hope that Christ may yet return to Russia in a manner different from such expectations.

Dostoevsky, like Kierkegaard, wanted a change of heart. The virtuous will have to grow humbler than they have been found to be; the sinners ought to find the fellowship they need. Human judgment must resign before God's wisdom. The rulers of state and Church everywhere must at long last open their cathedrals, Nietzsche's "sweet-smelling caves," and let Christ in, free to rule in Russia and everywhere. And the people, "these children," must learn to shoulder the heavy burden of freedom in order to experience how light the yoke can be. They must again want to become kings and not be satisfied with being couriers.

Next to Kierkegaard's challenge, Nietzsche's attack upon Christianity has been the most powerful blow against organized religion in recent European history. His exalted praise of suspicion as a force to bare the surface respectability of Christian society corresponds to Kierkegaard's aggressive condemnation and Dostoevsky's eerie panorama of Russian society. He rejects the claims of organized Christianity that it is a moralistic institution; he calls God "that which contradicts man." The fact that his philosophy of the superman was utilized in the creation of the subhuman standards of Nazi Germany and Italy was history's most impressive rejection of his self-exalting visions.

Germany remains Europe's greatest problem. Germany's past has never produced a political revolutionary. Luther as well as Marx were intellectual and spiritual leaders. Nietzsche's rebellion corroborates the impression that the German passion for extremes produces the perennial brooding over problems such as, "What is German?" This lack of measure and balance explains the German craving for discipline and the philosophical outcry for action that has made all revolutions not much more than a noisy search for a new ruler, as Ortega y Gasset calls them. Nietzsche is the embodiment of these excessive traits, together with the boldness of thought that is the genius of the Germans. Like Goethe, Hölderlin, and Schopenhauer, he was critical of the Germans to the point of contempt; yet Germany remained the center of his longing.

Germany will never lead the nations in political wisdom. Her genius lies in the world of philosophical and religious thinking. During the last century she was the leading nation in the various theological disciplines that have changed the face of modern Christianity everywhere. But she has also produced some of the most disturbing religious and anti-religious systems of thought that have ever migrated into the psychology of other nations. And it was her tragic fate to have given to the world a thinker of the rank of Nietzsche, who never tired of repeating that God had died.

André Malraux has asked the question whether man in the twentieth century can survive after God has died in the nineteenth century. His question has become mankind's greatest anxiety at a time when the genius for fission is our outstanding trait.

Only for those who are unwilling to risk the never-ending experiment of faith and who have even lost the pagan stoicism of Nietzsche, can Kafka's despair be the answer. His and some existentialists' delight in portraying evil and nothingness as the ultimate destiny is another fall of man away from the Christian call to transcend weakness and fear by faith. This negative harmony in man himself is a sign of moral exhaustion that needs to be interpreted as one more serious symptom of society's illness.

Were Kierkegaard, Dostoevsky, and Nietzsche born too early, as it has been said of them?

To their contemporaries they were a contradiction, an offense, but also a sign. Their living presence is the meaningful gift to our generation. They could arise only in a period for which their message came too early in order to speak to us who must see to it that their message does not come too late.

Is the angel's finger upon us?

Selected Bibliography for Further Reading

Selected Bibliography for Further Reading

Existentialism, by Ralph Harper. Cambridge, 1948. An excellent introduction with references to Kierkegaard, Heidegger, Sartre, Barth, Kafka, Dostoevsky, and others.

A Short History of Existentialism, by Jean Wahl. New York, 1949. A brief sketch of the philosophies of Heidegger, Kierkegaard, and Jaspers. This translation omits the study of indirect communication in Kierkegaard and Kafka which the French original contains.

Either/Or, by Sören Kierkegaard. Translation by D. F. Swenson, Lilian M. Swenson, and Walter Lowrie. 2 vols. Princeton, 1944. Basic for an understanding of Kierkegaard.

Training in Christianity and the Edifying Discourse which Accompanied It, by Sören Kierkegaard. Translation by Walter Lowrie. Princeton, 1945.

For Self-Examination and Judge for Yourself and Three Discourses, translation by Walter Lowrie. Princeton, 1945.

Kierkegaard's Attack upon Christendom, translation and introduction by Walter Lowrie. Princeton, 1944. Walter Lowrie's work is a lasting monument to his pioneering scholarship.

Purity of Heart, by Sören Kierkegaard. Translation by Douglas V. Steere. New York, 1948. A book of meditations.

Kierkegaard Anthology, edited by Robert Bretall. Princeton, 1947.

Kierkegaard, the Melancholy Dane, by H. V. Martin. New York, 1950. A brief and appealing introduction.

Kierkegaard; His Life and Thought, by E. L. Allen. New York (n.d.). A concise study with biographical emphasis.

Kierkegaard, the Cripple, by Theodor Haecker. New York, 1950. Excellent collection of portraits. Otherwise verbose and hypothetical.

Dostoevsky's complete works have been published in a 12-volume edition by Macmillan, New York. Translation by Constance Garnett.

Dostoevsky's "The Grand Inquisitor" has been published in a special reprint as a Haddam House Book with sensitive wood engravings by Fritz Eichenberg. Association Press, 1948.

The Diary of a Writer, by F. M. Dostoevsky. 2 vols. New York, 1949.

Dostoevsky, by Nicholas Berdyaev, New York, 1946. The outstanding religious interpretation.

Dostoevski. The Making of a Novelist, by Ernest J. Simmons. New York, 1940. Excellent background material of a general character.

Fyodor Dostoevsky, by René F. Miller. New York, 1950. Brief introduction for new readers.

Fyodor Dostoevsky, by J. A. T. Lloyd, New York, 1947. Pleasantly written, largely literary study.

Dostoevsky, by Janko Lavrin. New York, 1947. Summarizing his chief works.

Nietzsche, by Walter A. Kaufmann. Princeton, 1950. The most complete and up-to-date study in American literature, containing also an excellent bibliography.

Nietzsche, by Crane Brinton. Cambridge, 1941. A biographical study attempting an analysis of Nietzsche's thinking and his influence upon the Nazis. Sarcastic in tone.

The Philosophy of Nietzsche. Modern Library Giant, New York. Contains his chief works. *Thus Spake Zarathustra* is also available in the Modern Library.

Franz Kafka: A Biography, by Max Brod. New York, 1947.

The Kafka Problem, edited by Angel Flores. New York, 1947.

Kafka's Complete Works have been published by the Schocken Publishers, New York, in German and English editions.

Index of Names and Places

Index of Names and Places